Breaking Chains

Hope for Addicts
and Their Families

By: Paul C. Aragon
CDAC I, R.A.S., CSAC I, CSAC II, Recovery
Coach Cert.

I dedicate this book to:

My wife Shannon – When everyone told you to turn and run from me as fast as you can, you stood by me, and you believed in me. I thank you with all of my heart for all your support. Your faith in *Our Father* is amazing. Your strength as a *Christian Woman* and as a wife and as a mother is above the rest!! You are my *Angel* and my *Queen!!*
I Love You with All of my Heart!!

Shawna Dee, my firstborn child – I love you more than words could ever express. I apologize with all my heart for not being there as much as I should have been in your earlier years. I dedicate the chapter "Children Caught in the Wreckage of Addiction" to you!! Just know that daddy loves you so much!! XXX & OOO'z

Amanda and Tristan – I apologize for all the pain I have caused. You both are always in my heart. I love you!!

Breaking Chains ~ Paul Aragon

Paul Jr., Jacob and Rachael – Daddy loves you so much and I am so proud to be your daddy. I love you with all of my heart!!
Say no to drugs!!

My brother Skip – Thank you for all our Bible studies from thousands of miles away and for always believing in your little brother!! Thank you for leading me to our Father many years ago. Your love and leadership as my brother and as a man of God is so appreciated, and our Father has many gifts for you in heaven for all you do!

Preface

If you are a counselor, a therapist, a drug addict, the family or friend of a drug addict; if you struggle with depression or know someone who does, let me just say that *everyone* needs to read *Breaking Chains*. Paul's heart crushing life experiences are so realistically laid out in Chapter 1 in a way that anyone could relate to on some level.

In Chapter 2, he lays out the trauma caused on the family of a drug addict in an open-hearted and raw-to-the-core way. These two fast moving chapters take Paul through many years; and since recovery, he has had extensive schooling and experience in drug counseling.

I was asked to proofread this book, and I have got to say that Paul has become so much more than a drug counselor. As you enter Chapter 3, you will learn about drug addiction and so much more. You will learn about yourself, whoever you are. Paul has a gift you will quickly recognize. He can lay out the facts in a way that you've never heard before. I don't cry easily and this book has run me out of tears. What a gift he has! Everyone can learn from this book.

I have spent many years of my life on drugs and in prison. I, too, have wasted the first half of my life and hurt so many. In my 24 years of freedom from drugs and depression, I have never heard such healing words as the ones you will find in these pages. I wish I had this book a long time ago in my recovery, but it's here now.

If you are a counselor or therapist, do yourself one huge favor. Read this book. Paul is pro counselor, pro therapist, and pro 12 step recovery. Adding this book to your knowledge base will in some huge way change the way you look at things.

If you are a drug addict and you are reading this book right now, hold on for dear life my friend. I wish you well.

If you need a miracle, read *Breaking Chains*.

Skip Aragon

Table of Contents

Breaking Chains ~ Paul Aragon

Chapter 1

Demons in the Desert

It was a warm summer evening. The sun was about an hour from going down and the cravings were strong. There was no way I would make it through the night. Most dealers don't sell in the morning. They usually open up shop around noon at the earliest. "I need to get me some," I thought. "Just enough to get me through." I was in early withdrawals and needed to feel normal again. My body was sick and I needed a pick-me-up to help me function for the day.

On my way to score at my drug dealer's house, I ran into a friend at a gas station. I had seen this friend on the local news just a few hours prior. He was on the "valley's most wanted" local program. He saw me and seemed to be in a hurry when I told him he was all over the news. He was a meth cook. He told me he was leaving town and needed money. I told him I only had twenty dollars, and he offered me a big rock of freshly cooked meth for the twenty dollars in my pocket.

I took the dope and went out in the middle of the desert to party alone, like I always did. The rock of meth was a little smaller than golf ball, and I sat there and partied my heart out. Eventually, I began to see shadow monsters running from bush to bush. I heard the voices, clear as day of (what I believe) were demons talking to me. It has been many years since that day and I can't remember what they were saying to me, but I know that the words were harsh and demeaning. Those voices taunted me. I am not sure how, but the voices were clear. There was one voice in particular that I will never forget to this day. I had heard its voice in the past. It was deep and powerful. It spoke as if it had authority. It would also speak to the other voices as well, directing them. Sometimes it would defend me and sometimes it would order them to say and do things to upset me. It was obvious to me that they wanted more than just to toy with a drug addict. They wanted more. They wanted me! Oftentimes, they would tempt me with thoughts of suicide. I would challenge them; and when I did, it seemed to make things worse for me.

I got out of my truck that night and chased them through the desert, shouting, "I'm not afraid of you!" I could see their dark shadows lurking, but I couldn't get close enough to them. They would flee. I wasn't afraid of them. I wanted to fight. I ran so far and so long that night that by morning my truck was no where in sight. I began to walk back, unsure of my direction. Stopping for breakfast with my pipe in hand, the voices were still screaming all around; snarling at me. So many voices I couldn't keep up. I remember one specific voice that told me that I was going to "pay the piper." I had heard this before when I was high, but I had no idea what was going to happen to me. I did know that whenever I heard this particular voice say those words, something bad always happened; and it always happened quickly. I think that was one way the voices let me know they were real.

Not too long before this night, I heard that same demonic voice telling me I was going to "pay the piper." In less than a half hour I was pulled over and hauled off to jail. The voices I heard seem to have different roles, but there was always one that was in charge of all the demons (I believe) that were with me.

So I continued walking through the desert waiting to "pay the piper." It wasn't long until I almost stepped on a four and a half foot Mojave

[14]

Green rattlesnake, one of the deadliest snakes in the U.S. Its girth was enormous and its length stretched far. The rattles seemed to echo through the core of my mind, loud enough to hurt my ears. The snake was coiled and reared up looking straight at me. Its tongue flickered in and out of its mouth. Its color was slimy green and its head was poised to attack. I screamed at it. I yelled at the top of my lungs, "Is this all you've got for me!?" I kept screaming, but it never budged. It zoned in on my movements, tail rattling and tongue flickering, as if moving to a demonic beat. After I calmed down I sat down in the sand in front of it and smoked another bowl of meth. That snake never moved an inch. It was focused on me. I was sitting in the sand about four feet away; just me, the snake, my meth, and the demons lurking in the shadows.

I finished my bowl and stood up. I felt daring. I looked around, found a stick and began to tease the snake. I started yelling at it again and it became even more furious with me. I kept pinning its head to the ground with the stick and when my bravery kicked in, I grabbed it by the back of the neck. The snake was much heavier than it looked. Its mouth was open and its huge fangs were seething to taste my blood. The venom from the

Breaking Chains ~ Paul Aragon

Mojave Green can incapacitate a person within 20 minutes and cause death within an hour. There was no way I was making it out of the desert alive if it bit me.

With snake in hand, I screamed again at those demons that stalked me from the bushes. I choked the snake, squeezing as hard as I could. There was no way I could let it go. I had to kill it. I needed to show those demons I wasn't afraid. I picked up a rock and began to beat on the end of the tail. I wanted the rattles as a trophy. There were 12 rattles in all. He was a so large it seemed to take forever getting those rattles; but they finally broke off and I stuck the rattles in my pocket.

It didn't take long for the snake to die; I was squeezing its neck mercilessly. Once dead, I threw it to the ground and screamed in victory at those demons whose voices seemed to dissipate into the night air.

I began walking to find my truck; however, I still couldn't find it. I stopped from time to time to light up my bowl. The night moved quickly and by morning I had walked past my truck-again. By this time I had no idea how long I had been out there, in the desert. I was thirsty more than anything; and knew that if I could just find my truck, there was a bottle of water waiting for me.

Finally I saw my truck in the distance. I never realized that chasing demons could be this stupid. But their voices were so clear that something deep inside me had to find out if they were in fact truly real.

It was days before I returned home to my wife. She was about done with me; I mean could I blame her? She asked where I had been and I told her my truck broke down. She didn't believe me. My eyes told the truth: I looked like death. I had been up for days. Of course I blamed her for my disappearance because I started an argument before I even left, just so I had an excuse to leave and get high. Addicts blame everyone but themselves for their addiction.

I argued with her and she yelled at me. She was done with me, I knew it. I managed to calm her down and told her I would stop for good. Another promise I knew I would break before I ever got clean. I was just buying more time to use. So she sent me off to bed.

Night had set in by the time I got home. I turned the lights off in my room and lay down on my bed. I knew I wasn't going to sleep though. I could hear the TV in the front room knowing my wife was waiting for me to fall asleep. I couldn't sleep. I had smoked so much meth that I was hearing the voices again in full force. I could hear them out my window. I could hear voices in my front room talking to my wife, telling her to leave me. I got up and peeked through the door. No one was there. Was my mind playing tricks on me? I lay down and tried ignoring all the voices. The voices I heard outside were so clear. The shadow monsters engulfed my room like never before. I heard aliens on the roof; I could hear them: "Rat a tat tat Rat a tat tat," all over my roof. They seemed to be everywhere.

I said in a quiet but stern voice, "Better get the fuck off my roof or I'll shoot you off." Then it was silent. I heard it again, "Rat a tat tat, Rat a tat tat" across my roof. I reached into my closet from my bed and pulled out my L-500 Mossberg. I pulled the pin out and stuck seven rounds in the chamber. I waited. I heard it again "Rat a tat tat" scampering across my roof.

BAM! BAM!

I unloaded all seven shots into the ceiling in my bedroom. My wife came in the room and turned on the light,

"What the hell are you doing!?" she yelled.

"I am cleaning my gun," I told her.

Breaking Chains ~ Paul Aragon

"Cleaning your gun with the lights off and bullets in the chamber? I am done, I am leaving you," she said.

I got up and shook the ceiling off my blankets and lay there staring at the holes in my ceiling. Two weeks later my wife left me, moved out of state, never to see or talk to me again.

With my wife gone I managed to put the drugs down for a while. I was living in the home alone and was regretful for what I had done to her. I managed to get clean for a few months but it wasn't enough to get my wife back, she was gone. During those two months I met, who years later would be, my third wife. A woman who I would put through more hell than the first two wives' combined. A woman who would try her hardest to stick by me until enough was enough.

I was on a roll destroying nice sweet women, whom I truly loved. I am not sure why but I always managed to attract good-looking women who never messed with drugs. I would shake and rattle them in my drug addiction. I would use them until they couldn't handle the pain and destruction caused by my drug addiction.

They were beautiful loving women who wanted nothing more than to love me and spend their life with me, only to find out later that they fell in love with a drug addict that couldn't find a way to get clean. I couldn't manage to fight the cravings that were buried deep inside me.

You may be wondering why I started this book with this story. I think it is so important that if you are going to heal that you see all sides of addiction and what goes on in an addict's world.

This is only one story, but there are more within these pages. I could never imagine what a loved one goes through even though I have seen what it has done. I haven't been in their shoes. I do know that in order to combat addiction we have to look at even the darkest places, so we are prepared to deal with the tragic destruction of loved ones by the selfish antics of an addict.

Upon reading this story, many people may think paranoia, awake too long, and the drugs are why I saw demons in the desert. That would be the most logical reason for anyone and quite possible. Demons are something most addicts won't talk about because they are considered fantasy or hallucinations.

Not only do meth addicts go through this, but many drugs have the same effects. FBI agents outside, cops are watching you, people are following you, people are talking about you. These are from the paranoia that follows with using drugs, even marijuana.

Many of my colleagues in the substance abuse field would label me crazy for even suggesting that there are spiritual things that take place in the eyes of an addict, or in their addiction. Other colleagues will stay quiet and keep their opinion to themselves because of an experience that still holds a place in their memory.

I have never been the kind of person to hide what I feel and know in my heart. What better place for a demon to show itself than in a vulnerable moment in our addiction? No one will believe it and that's why most addicts won't speak of it. It's the perfect crime. Drive a man to the edge of insanity with no detection. It's just the drugs, science would tell us, and it's plausible. If God is among us, answering prayers and guiding us, how perfect is it for demons to appear through the poison burning in our veins? Makes sense to me. Besides, I know what I saw and what I have seen. No one can take from me what I know in my heart.

So why is this so important to discuss? Because it's addiction, and with addiction we must look at all aspects of what goes on in the life on an addict.

Breaking Chains ~ Paul Aragon

Either way you need to know everything you're in for, whether you're an addict reading this book or a loved one of the addict.

Family members of addicts, including my own wife, say: there is pure evil in an addict when they are deep into their addiction. I have heard loved ones also say that they have felt an evil presence in their house even when the addict wasn't there. Many people feel that the addiction brings darkness into the home.

So how is this book helpful in bringing hope to families while speaking of darkness? Because where there is darkness, light will always supersede. What I mean is this: darkness is the absence of light. When it is dark we turn on the light. Within the pages of this book I will show you how to turn that light on, and that light is found in the power of love.

Never Too Broken

Every time I breathed,
I felt the demons moving inside me.
I couldn't break free from the insanity,
As I pushed those I love further from me.
The fire in my veins,
The addiction inside me,

It was too much for me to break free,
From the chains that bind me.
The rage inside my head,
So many times I wished myself dead.
I could feel the demons scratching at me,
Broken thoughts of who I could be,
There was a broken man inside me.
Trying to mask the fear,
I couldn't hold onto the things I held dear.
The two faces I had was a lie.
The one said, smile,
The other said, cry.
I fought so hard for the one fix,
But my addiction was one big trick.
It never came.
Addiction is a thief.
It took everything I owned.
Everything I loved.
I needed a hero.
But no one could save me.
It had to be me.
To work for, what my heart so desired.
That was the only way it would have meaning.
That would be the only way, I could embrace that
change.
And it all started,
On my knees

Poem by Paul C. Aragon

Chapter 2

Children Caught in the Wreckage of Addiction

I met my first wife at the age of 22 years old; we married six months later. She was an awesome lady who helped me fulfill my dream of having a child of my own. She gave me my firstborn child, a beautiful little girl. I named her Shawna. She was the most beautiful little girl any daddy could ever ask for. She quickly became daddy's little girl. I loved holding her in my arms. I hated going to work every day because I would have to leave her. Holding her was the first thing I did when I came home. She would look in my eyes and know that she was the most precious thing in my life. I loved it when she would fall asleep on my chest.

My wife made me promise, when we first got together, that I would never do hard drugs. She promised to be a good wife to me as long as I never brought hard drugs back into my life. She told me that it would only take one slip-up and our life together would be over. She didn't mind if I smoked pot once in a while but hard drugs would not be accepted in our life together.

She was a good wife, hardworking and a very good mother to my baby girl. That little girl was in my arms every minute I was home. I was tremendously in love with my family.

I had my own painting company at the age of 24 and bought a new house. Watching the house be built on the top of a hill was more than I ever expected from this runaway-child-turned-gang-banger-drug-addict. It was a dream come true life for me. I came from a very bad childhood of gangs and drugs and juvenile halls and jails, but when I met my wife my world changed. I never dreamed of the life I had, yet it would all end too quickly.

I hired a man to work for me and I had no idea he used drugs. My business was thriving and I was working seven days a week to provide for my family. We were on our way home from a job and I remember telling him how tired I was one day. He mentioned that he had some meth at his house. I was so tired I just didn't even think. He offered some to me and I said ok. I only did a very small line, but it kept me up for three days. I remember being so burned out when it wore off that I needed more to keep going.

Breaking Chains ~ Paul Aragon

This went on for about three months. I felt so guilty I knew I had to stop, and I did. My wife and I were having financial difficulties at the time and weren't getting along too well. I felt so guilty that one day I told her about my drug use months prior. I hadn't currently been using (for about two months) when I told her. She didn't forget what she said five years earlier and that was it: we were over. It seemed my dream life was gone as fast as it started.

I was young and I was stupid and I paid the price for it. I cried when I moved out. It was devastating for me to leave my wife with whom I loved so much and my beautiful two year old baby girl. I tried to reconcile. It was over. It didn't take long for me to go back to the one thing that dismantled my family in the first place. I started using every day and my business quickly started crumbling.

I visited my daughter every weekend and even visited her during the week. But it didn't take long for it to turn into weeks before I would see her. I tried visiting her every other weekend but my addiction took over everything.

Years passed by and my daughter grew up quickly. She had moved to another county, making it difficult to see her. I missed out on so much of her life. I was grateful that she wasn't there to see my addiction grip a hold of me in full force. I was grateful that she had been protected from me and my addiction. When she visited me I spent time with my baby girl, but it wasn't as often as I should. The guilt still haunts me to this day. I missed out on many years in my little girl's life. I will never get those years back. My daughter and I have a great relationship now. She loves her daddy with all of her heart and she has forgiven me for not being the dad I should have been during her younger years; it is an emotional scar I will live with for the rest of my life.

Addiction is like an F-5 tornado. After the devastation you look back at the wreckage wondering how you will ever recover. This leads many addicts to sink back into their addiction so they don't feel the pain; so they don't have to come to terms with the wreckage they caused.

The worst part of all the wreckage caused by addiction is the effect it has on children. Addicts, including me, bring children into this world with no concept of what it means to be a parent. The kids are neglected and grow up following in the footsteps of the addicted parent. I was blessed to have a wife who didn't use drugs, and my child was saved, and for the most part removed, from that part of my life.

Children of addicts suffer because they are not given the attention needed to feel safe and stable. They are underfed and wear the same clothes day after day. Their hygiene is ignored and they grow up in a world of chaos. The sad part is that these children think that their life is normal and that all kids grow up this way. It isn't until later in life that they realize their world is anything but normal. Mom and dad sleep for countless hours while the children have to fend for themselves by fixing their own meals, and usually what they make isn't what society would consider healthy eating. The addicted parents have other addicts over to party and the kids feel unsafe in their own home.

Many children are removed from their homes by children's services and put into foster care. The only requirement for the children to return home is for the parents to get into treatment for their drug addiction. They have to show the state that they are rehabilitated and can take care of their child again. Believe it or not, many parents won't go to treatment or they just can't manage to stay clean long enough for the child to return home. Most children blame themselves. They grow up with the idea that it was their fault and that they are bad kids. This can start a whole new cycle and a new generation of addicted children.

Usually the kids are put into the care of the grandparents or other family members. This can be tough on the children while enabling the parents to continue in their addiction. The kids are essentially still in their care and they can see the kids whenever they want; but they neglect that opportunity as well and use it as free rein to get high. They think the kids are ok because grandma and grandpa are taking care of them. The grandparents end up raising the kids, while the parents continue their spree of addiction. Then, when the grandparents refuse to let the addict see their children, resentment takes its roots. The grandparents become the bad people and the addict blames everyone but themselves for the kids being taken from them in the first place.

The primary reason the kids are taken from the home is that the parents just can't seem to stop getting high. The addict, however, won't see that. All they see is that the grandparents or other family members are bad because they won't let them see the kids. They really believe that the grandparents are responsible for their kids or that the grandparents should just ignore the state and let the children return home to addicted parents.

This burden is put on many family members such as grandparents, aunts, uncles, brothers, sisters and even family friends. Many times an addict goes to jail and expects the family members to bail them out. One more problem caused by their addiction. Many parents feel guilty and will bail their addicted loved one out of jail or give them money or buy their food. They continue to enable the addict's bad behavior because they hope that this time the addicted one is serious about getting clean. Usually they never do. Thousands of dollars are spent trying to help their loved one get off drugs so they can be a parent to their children. But promise after promise is broken, yet the family members keep trying to help their loved one get off their addiction. They never give up hope.

I can tell you that it is understandable for a mother or father to help their child, but the truth is they can't. I have had many people ask me how they can help their loved one get off drugs so the family can reunite and the kids can return home. I said it before and I will say it again: *you can't help them*. Recovery has to be what the addict truly desires in their heart in order to recover from addiction. The more you try to help them, the more you are keeping them from recovery. They will never hit their rock bottom because you are preventing them from doing so every time you bail them out of a problem.

In the substance abuse field we call this *enabling the addict*. You are enabling them to continue their bad behavior. Tough love is usually the best way to deal with an addicted loved one. You can cheer them on and love them, but set boundaries and let them find their own way.

You have to decide what is best for the kids and their future. Is it smart to let an addicted loved one come over to visit the kids when you know in your heart they are not clean and sober? Is it healthy for the addicted parent to drop by to visit the kids every few weeks or every few months with no consistency? The answer is that it is not healthy. The parents leave and continue their addiction while the children are left crying and wondering when they will see their parents again. The kids know that they won't see them for a while because that is the pattern. The kids will be fine in their new life with you and then months later the addicted parent drops by and the kid is sent into turmoil again. Who has to deal with that turmoil? You do! The addicted parent has no idea the pain they are leaving in the wake of their addiction and in the wake of their inconsistency as a parent.

Let's look at this from another angle in which the kids are in the care of an addicted parent when drug dealers come over to the house. The addict doesn't realize they are putting that child in danger. Many addicts will even bring their children to the drug dealer's house just to get their dope. They will either leave their child in the car unattended or they will bring them into a house filled with the smell of drugs. Then they go home and hide away to get high while the children are left unattended and to fend for themselves. Many addicts will say they were only gone for a moment, not realizing how much time actually passed. When I was using drugs, time passed by so quickly; what seemed like minutes, turned into hours or days. Drug addicts lose track of time while high. All sense of responsibility leaves and the only thing important is getting high.

Many children are put in harm's way more often than not. Sexual, physical and mental abuse not only comes from the addicted parents but also from the addicts that come over to the house. Many children are bartered for drugs and used for sexual favors. Most people understand this but drugs, to an addict, are first and foremost in their life.

Does this happen with all addicts? No, but it happens more often than most care to admit. So why am I sharing this with you? If you are a parent and your opposite parent is using drugs and you're allowing it in the home, not only can the addict can be arrested, but you can be arrested as well for putting your child in danger. If you have knowledge that your spouse is using and DHS finds out, or something tragic happens without your knowledge, you can be charged with child neglect and child endangerment. Many parents with a drug addicted spouse never think that their husband or wife would ever do anything to put their child in danger; but with drugs in their system, that addict they love isn't in their natural state of mind. Their mind has been altered and their thinking is irrational. They can and will put those children in harm's way.

So how does all this affect the child? I can tell you from personal experience in my own addiction. My wife didn't use drugs, I was that addicted parent. I harmed my kids simply by the withdrawals. That was the extent of the harm I did to my family. Doesn't sound too bad, does it? Well it was.

When I was coming down off dope I was constantly causing arguments and fights with my wife, and the kids were usually always in the room. I was constantly yelling and screaming at my wife, and it would always end with me being kicked out of the house. How do you think that affects the kids? I would yell at the kids and the dog and everyone in the house and think that it was normal. Then two weeks later when I returned home, it would happen all over again.

The kids begin to think this is normal and that isn't healthy. The boys begin to think that this is how you treat women and they grow up doing the same, even without drugs. The sad part is that my wife was always the bad guy in the eyes of my children because she kicked me out of the house. Dad is gone and it's mom's fault. Kids don't understand addiction and you can't expect them to; they are kids. The only things they should understand are that the color blue is blue and that one plus one is two. Addiction is too much for a little child to take in.

If you're reading this book and you are in a situation with a spouse on drugs, kick them out and don't let them return until they can show you that they are clean and working on some kind of program to stay clean. If you're an addict and reading this book, you may despise me for giving that advice, but I know addiction. I have been there. I will always say that kids come first and should be protected at all cost. After I returned home with "clean time" my wife always kept a drug test kit on hand. If she thought that I was out of character in anyway, she would tell me to pee in a cup, and she would watch me pee in the cup because addicts are cunning people.

A clean addict in recovery will NEVER have a problem peeing in a cup. However, an addict that is using will say and do anything not to comply. They will say things like "What? You don't trust me?" They will do everything possible, even telling you they can't pee right now, to keep from taking that test. Then, two days later, when they are clean they will volunteer to take the test. This might help you:

1. Meth will stay in the system between 2 and 4 days depending on the size of the addict and the tolerance level.
2. Marijuana will stay in the system up to 36 days depending on the tolerance level and size of the user.
3. Crack cocaine will stay in the system between 2 and 4 days depending on the size of the user and the tolerance level.

Breaking Chains ~ Paul Aragon

4. Heroin will stay in the system between 2 and 4 days depending on the size of the user and the tolerance level.

5. Opiates (oxycodone, vicodine, and valium) will stay in the system 2 to 4 days depending on the tolerance level, quantity taken and the size of the user.

Many addicts will argue and tell you that this chart isn't accurate, but it is accurate in most cases. They may tell you things like, "I ate some poppy seed bagels and that's why I am positive for opiates." In order get a positive test for opiates by eating poppy seeds you would have to eat a handful of poppy seeds, approximately 5 grams, and most people don't consume the amount it would take to get a positive test from poppy seeds. For instance, it would take a whole bag of poppy seed bagels to get a positive for opiates, and I don't know too many people who would consume that many bagels in one sitting. Some may say this isn't true, but a co-worker and I both tested it, trying to get the levels it would take to test positive.

They may also say, "I took cough syrup and that is why I have a positive for meth or opiates." The truth is that they would have to consume an abnormal amount shortly before the test in order to test positive for meth or opiates.

If you ever suspect your spouse is using and want to be sure, buy the test that you can read in your own home and can mail the urine out to a lab. This way you can be sure if they are telling you the truth or a story. Then you can get the true results back a few days later by going to the website of the testing lab and punching in a security code.

Many addicts will do whatever they can to get their kids back, but many will not. Although this may sound drastic, tough love is what worked for me. No child should be required to live in a house with an active addict. Remember that DHS can take those kids from you for child endangerment or child neglect if you have them living in the house with an active user.

So what does a parent who truly wants the kids back and really wants to do the right thing do? The first thing they do is get clean. Make the decision to get and stay off drugs. You can also go to an outpatient program or possibly an inpatient program if you need more stringent and intense therapy. Try to find a program that works for you and work hard. Carry a picture of your kids with you at all times and when you feel the urge to use drugs, pull out that picture and remind yourself of what is most important in your life.

Some of the finest people I have ever met are addicts in recovery. They work so hard to change their lives and become new people who have an incredible amount of compassion and love. I also strongly suggest going to as many parenting classes as you can to learn how to be a role model for your kids. Learn what to say, how to act and how to respond to your kids. Learn how to disciple them. When DHS or the family members who are taking care of your kids see that you are changing your life, doors will open. Don't expect anyone to give you anything just because you're clean. Remember you have caused damage and it is going to take time for others around you to heal, including you.

Let your loved ones heal and don't expect everyone to heal right away because you're in recovery. Healing and gaining back trust may take a long time. Remember all the lies and all the broken promises that you told? Well, it's hard to forget easily. They need to see you off drugs and changing your life for a substantial amount of time.

Set up a time and day every week, as often as possible, to visit your kids; make sure it is convenient for those taking care of them. Be consistent and be on time. Make the most of your time during visits, letting your children know they are the most important aspect of your life. Read books to them or play a game with them. Let the children see your gratitude towards the people who have been taking care of your kids. Make amends to them and follow through with calling your kids every day or every other day. Check with the people taking care of the kids and ask if you can start calling them and what time would be best. If they deny you anything just say, "I understand I have more work to do and I am willing to do what it takes." Say it with a smile and with compassion because of the choices you have made. Try to really see from your heart the damage you have caused. If you have trouble with that, then I strongly suggest you try the 12 steps.

Get a sponsor to take you through the steps so you can see the damage you have caused and find the change for you to be a new creation to those who knew you. People will see change in you before you do. Work hard at it and the rewards will be so great for you and your children.

Give your kids the time it takes to heal from the pain; they have earned it. Many times, I have seen children that never speak to their parents again because too many years were wasted in addiction rather than trying to be a parent. Don't let those years slip by. If they do, never stop trying to let your kids know you love them. Continue to try and prove yourself worthy of their love by staying off drugs and changing yourself from the inside out.

Lastly, I would encourage you to believe in yourself and never give up, no matter how hard it gets. Your children are gifts from something much bigger than you and I. You have been given those kids by grace. Cherish and honor that. Become the person that everyone knows you can be. Do it for you and enjoy being a responsible and loving parent.

Those kids of yours are counting on you!

Dear God
Where is my daddy?
Did I do something wrong?
He never visits me.
I love being with my daddy.
God, is my daddy ok?
I wish he would call me.
I wish he would spend time with me.
I remember my daddy taught me to ride a bike.
I was so scared, but he helped me.
I wish I could help my daddy.
I wish I could hug him.
I wish he could kiss me goodnight.
I miss my daddy so much.
God, does my daddy think of me?
He doesn't call me very much.
My mommy gets mad at him.
My friends always ask me about my daddy.
I tell them he is a good daddy.
Sometimes I see him.
He cries a lot when he says goodbye.
Is it because he won't see me for a while?
My mommy and daddy aren't together anymore.
I think my daddy did something wrong.
God could you give my daddy a hug for me?
Tell him I love him.
Please take care of my daddy.
Amen.

Poem by Paul C. Aragon

Chapter 3

Repairing the Damage from Your Addiction

The toughest hurdle every addict faces in their recovery is repairing the damage with those they love, cleaning up all the debt owed to others, and trying to live a life they haven't lived in years, possibly ever.

In this chapter I will try to touch on all these issues that present themselves in recovery. The 12 steps, as I have said, address these issues specifically; and I recommend them to anyone that is seeking thorough change in their life.

Addicts cause so much damage in their addiction that the cleanup is equivalent to an F-5 tornado roaring through town after town with devastation. The addict roars through the lives of person after person leaving a wake of destruction without blinking an eye. Addicts are selfish, self-centered, dishonest and inconsiderate. Addicts only think about how and where to get their next fix. Parents try desperately to see where they went wrong and where they can help their lost child, but everywhere they turn is another disappointment. Mom hasn't had a full night's sleep in weeks waiting for her child to call and let her know they're ok. Dad is a wreck watching his wife fall apart. Being the man, anger sets in, wanting to protect his wife from hurt that is delivered by the addicted child. This is like two magnets turned against each other, they just won't join together. The marriage that was once strong now begins to weaken.

One parent says, "We must do everything we can to help our child." The other parent says, "They are an adult now. Let them figure it out on their own." This can push the family further apart, while the addicted son/daughter is in someone's house getting high and not even thinking of their parents or kids if there are any.

When there is communication, the addict blames mom and dad for not giving them money or not helping meet their needs or wants. There is yelling and screaming within the family and it always ends with the addict blaming everyone for their addiction except the person they see in the mirror.

Items end up missing from the house: jewelry, money, electronics, antiques or anything the addict can squeeze down their pants or tuck in their jacket to buy another hit.

In my earlier years of addiction, I found my step dad's war medals in a drawer. He had many of them. I took them all out of the cases and sold them to a local pawn shop for money so I could buy drugs. My step dad was devastated when he found his priceless medals gone, and he knew that I was the one who took them. He begged and pleaded with me to tell him where they were and that he wouldn't get mad, that he just wanted his medals that had more memories than I could ever fathom. I finally told him the name of the pawn shop and he had to buy them back at a more costly price. He would never speak to me again.

How could I have no compassion for him and his well-earned medals?

I will tell you why: Addiction is not just some word that floats around from person to person. Addiction is alive and it will consume the person you knew and turn them into something evil. It will steal their heart and soul, and turn them inside out. It will `do it so quickly that the addicts will never know what hit them. They are lost in a delusional world where everyone is wrong and they are always right, and everyone is out to get them and they are causing no harm to anyone but themselves. Seeing evil in the eyes of their addicted loved one in the midst of countless arguments makes parents fearful. Where did this come from? I have been an addict for many years and I can honestly tell you it comes straight from the pit of hell. It is not your child you are fighting, it is someone else.

Let's talk about the wife or husband with the spouse that is on drugs and has been doing so under their noses for quite some time. They have been doing things you never could have thought possible: sleeping with other people for money or drugs, selling items from around the home and taking money from the bank account. The sober spouse rummages through a tool box or a jewelry box and finds drugs and paraphernalia. The user promises they will stop and time after time they are caught using again. This repeats itself over and over and over. They both have kids and she/he now feels responsible to help the using spouse until they finally get and take help. You may want to pack a bag or a lunch because you might be waiting a long time.

But let's say the non-using spouse took my advice and kicked them out until they got clean.

Too much time has passed and the spouse kept using drugs. The marriage slipped away into a pool full of tears and broken promises, and children who are caught in the middle.

If this addict is you or if you are the non-addicted spouse, I have good news. Healing can take place for both of you whether you are together or not.

Can any addict or parent or spouse reading this relate to some of these things that I have shared? I am sure many of you can. I have good news for you, too. There is a kind and compassionate person inside, but the removal of drugs won't be the only thing necessary for the return of your loved one. Removing the drugs will only remove a symptom of the problem. Addicts must reach down inside themselves and work hard to bring out the man or woman that God intentionally created, not the person drugs destroyed.

I would say to an addict reading this book that if you truly want to change your life and bring your loved ones close to you again, give your loved ones space. Take a certain amount of time away for yourself to work on you. Trying to convince everyone that you're serious this time about wanting to change is just blowing wind to them; the action is in the footwork. Trying to get everyone to see that you are clean, in recovery, and need their support is not a good idea. Aren't we this needy in our addiction?

You don't need their help. What you really need to do is to put your program together by yourself and show yourself that you are in this for the long haul. The family will think there are ulterior motives if you're trying to show them how awesome you are for having a few days in recovery. Don't get me wrong. One day is a miracle, but your family needs time to heal.

What better way is there to heal than for your family to see you clean once in a while and to hear your clean and sober voice when you call them? Don't call bragging about how many days you have; keep that between you and your peers in recovery. If they ask, you can tell them, but always keep the conversation about them and their life. It will be refreshing for them to be the center of conversation and the center of attention like you have been for so many years. It will be so refreshing for them to know your desire to hear about their life.

Answer questions about you briefly, but always let them see you changing the conversation and making it about their life, which will show them you are trying to change. Back off and give your loved ones time. Let the wounds heal for a period of at least six months while you really work on you.

You have heard the saying:

Hate the addiction,

Hate the drugs,

Pray for the addict.

This is true. Addiction is a monster and has the ability to destroy families with the sweep of its hand. Drugs are found everywhere in this world and seem to destroy every hand they touch. Repairing the damage caused by drugs can take many years to do. Some damage caused by drugs can be so bad that there is no repairing it. However, I always say that nothing is impossible when God is in the center of it.

It has been many years since I got clean and sober and I still am repairing damage done to those that I love and hold dear to my heart. You have heard that idle hands are the devil's workshop? Well, you can't expect people to come to know a new person if there is nothing new about you. Removing the drugs is only the first step. You have to work on every aspect of your life to change who you are or you will change nothing. My family saw me changing who I was.

Breaking Chains ~ Paul Aragon

When they were able to see that, they were able to come to a point where they could begin to trust me again.

Parenting classes, marriage counseling and even individual counseling helped me to set a path to change. I was then able to see what I had lacked in my life and what addiction stole from me. When I was able to see those things, then I was able to change my life. I still work hard on change. It will be a lifelong journey for me to be all that I know I can be, inside and out. Church every weekend, Bible studies, meetings, helping others, schools, trainings, workshops, therapy, volunteering at my church (just to name a few) are the things that help me change every day.

I try not to take things personally. The other day they were putting a new sign up at my church and I was trying to tell them how to center the sign. More than likely they would have centered the sign without my help. I had to look at why I needed to control that situation. Many of you are thinking that I was just trying to help and it is true. However, there were four other men there. Sometimes it goes deeper than trying to help and it becomes, "I need to control this situation."

I later sent a text to one of the men there and told him I was sorry for trying to control the situation. Of course he had no idea what I was saying and quickly said, "We love your heart." The heart they saw was a man trying to reach inside himself and see where he needed to change. The truth is that this world functions just fine without me. I don't need to control or be involved with everything. Those men planned on putting that sign up before I got there, they did it without me and it turned out great.

If you're trying to figure out my point here, my point is this: don't be afraid to look inside yourself and where you need to change. The man that I texted that day saw that I looked inside my heart and realized I was wrong to jump into what they were doing. So how did he respond to me? He said, "I love your heart." What he really said was that he loved that I could look inside myself, find change; and love was the result.

Do you want people to see you as a new person inside? Then you have to be willing to look inside yourself and change who you are on a daily basis. Change takes practice every day.

I have something you can try: try to go all day today with a smile on your face. Even when you're talking to people, do it with a smile. Watch how people react to you. You will hear things like, "How come you're so happy?" or "How come you're smiling so much?" People will notice that something changes in you just by holding a smile all day long. If you do it again tomorrow and the next day, then you will form a habit in smiling all day even when you talk. This is how people change: by creating healthy habits.

If you want people to see that you have changed your life, then you need to promote change. If your loved ones see you day in and day out, having seen you in your addiction, they should know you pretty well, right? Then they will be the first ones to see you changing your life. Change is what will bring them to forgive you and trust you again.

Let me share a story with you. When my wife kicked me out of the house and said never to return home, she was so broken. I hurt her so much that she was done with me. Repairing that damage was hard for me, but it was worth it considering what I have many years later. Everything I did in my recovery, especially the 12 steps, promoted change in me and my wife saw that change in me. When I went to her house to see my kids she sat me down and said, "I see something different in your eyes and in your smile. I have heard from so many people how you have changed and how wonderful of a man you have become in such a short period of time. I see that change and I want you to come home to me." My work paid off, yes it took months, but it paid off.

Sometimes people are lazy in their recovery. They assume that as soon as they get off drugs, everyone is supposed to bow at their feet, forgive them and tell them how wonderful they are because they have a few days off dope. DHS is supposed to bring the kids back, mom and dad should let you move back home and forget all that you have done; the wife is supposed to let you move back in and forget all the crap you put her through.

Here is the kicker: they get to watch you sit on your butt all day long watching TV and doing nothing all because you're off dope. "Let's bow down to the addict because he has a few days clean." It doesn't work that way.

If you want change and forgiveness, prove it. Work for it. Let them see you going to meetings, church, Bible studies, and men's/women's groups; working with your sponsor; going to school and/or getting a job; walking differently and responding differently; honest. Let them see all that, then watch how they respond.

Don't let an addict come home if they can't show you prior to coming home that they have changed. Don't just trust them and take their word for it. Know in your heart that they have changed and let their actions show it, not their words. Addicts need to prove that they are willing to work to get what their heart desires; you can't just give it to them. This is called tough love, and it is the love that saved my life and my marriage. Was it hard for my wife to follow through with that marriage? Yes! She will tell you that it was worth all the months of being a hard ass to me. Not only did it save my life but it saved our marriage.

Tough love can work because it forces the addict into doing what it takes to come home. However, it doesn't always work. Sometimes it pushes the addict further away because they think you have abandoned them. The truth is they're mad because they no longer have you to use and abuse anymore. It's leaving them without a source of money to buy their drugs and it pisses them off.

Addicts always blame someone else for their problems. They really believe with all their heart that it is someone else's fault and that their life is so bad because of someone else's issues. They will justify, rationalize and minimize their behavior because they refuse to see that the drugs have ruined their life and their relationships.

Another way to promote change is by changing the people we hang around. Many addicts want to hold on to the people they call their friends. When we change the people we hang around and implement positive people in our life, then we can potentially change faster. This is why I mention the entire thing that I did in the above paragraph about places that help change us. When we do those things I mentioned, we meet new people, and then they become a part of our life. So when our loved ones see us hanging out with people that are positive role models and the old friends are gone, then this is a very positive piece of change that they will notice quickly.

Repairing the damage does take time. The hardest part is getting past the first few weeks. I can promise you, if you jump out of the gate like a horse that wants to win the race, you will succeed quicker than you might realize. Trust and have faith that you are smart enough to change and you are worth the effort. However, that willingness to change must come from deep inside you and you must give your recovery everything inside of you.

If you are a loved one reading this book, give your addicted loved one time. Set boundaries and be supportive if they are showing you change. Don't try to do the work for them, let them do it on their own because their recovery holds more value in their hearts.

God gives us opportunity
When you pray for change....God won't give you change.
He will give you opportunity to change.
When you pray for help...God won't help you.
He will give you opportunity to be helped.
When you pray for wisdom....God won't give you wisdom.
He will give you opportunity to be wise.
When you pray for strength...God won't give you strength.
He will give you opportunity to obtain strength, and the opportunity to be strong.
When you pray for humility… God won't give you humility.
He will give you opportunity to practice humility.
Nothing comes without OPPORTUNITY for you to work for what you desire from God.
FAITH without work is dead FAITH.
When you pray for comfort.....GOD WILL COMFORT YOU.

Poem by Paul C. Aragon

Chapter 4

Why Do Addicts Turn to God in Recovery?

If you are atheist or agnostic I would ask you to continue reading this chapter. Read it with an open mind and an open heart. Aren't you trying to change your life and your way of thinking? If the answer is yes, then I would urge you to start here. In this chapter I will do my best in laymen's terms to answer questions you may have about this "God thing". In recovery there will be many things that we don't want to do and through my experience those are the things we need to do the most! I am not trying to convert anyone in this chapter, but I am trying to get you uncomfortable; because when we are uncomfortable in our recovery, we are changing. This is a good thing! If you are a person of faith I would ask you as well to continue reading to broaden your horizons on the topic of God.

I will not be quoting scriptures in this chapter because I don't want to derail or discourage anyone from reading this chapter. This is probably the most important chapter in this book; so I will explain in a personal and intimate way how this power that is greater than us can truly be an asset in our recovery if we are willing to receive it.

Many people have a problem believing in a God that they cannot see. If there is a God, why does he not show himself to us? This answer is simple. When God created us he wanted us to come to him out of love and out of faith. Faith is believing without seeing. Believe it or not, even believers have a hard time with this, they just don't admit it. If we saw God every day and God talked to each of us every day, there would be no faith needed in him. God wants us to come to him out of love, not because we know he is watching us at all times.

So if this God is so concerned about us and loves us so much, then why would he allow us to go through the hardships that we do? Why does he let bad things happen in this world? I can tell you I struggled with this so much in my earlier years. I was being physically abused as a child and sexually molested for many years. This is the reason I started using alcohol and drugs. I hated God for allowing me to go through these things when this Bible tells me over and over again that he is a God of love.

I cursed his name every moment I got, and blamed him for all that I went through. But when God made this planet and his children on it, he gave us "free will." This means that we could do and act any way that we wanted to act, and do to others anything that we wanted to do. So the person that beat me for so many years chose to do those things, and even though it hurt God to see those things done to his child, he didn't intervene.

The person that did those things to me would one day have to answer for those things and it wasn't my place to question why God chooses to do it this way. But I can say that he stands by those who come to him through faith. I found out recently that the man that sexually abused me was sent to prison for 15 years. I pray he finds God there. Does it still bother me why he chose to do horrible things to me and many other kids? Yes! It does bother me at times, but I have found it in my heart to forgive him for the things he did to me. Did I forgive him to his face? No. I don't think I could do that. But I have forgiven him through God's love that only he can provide. Because this world is a place of free will, many people will make bad choices that hurt others, and somehow they ALWAYS pay for what they have done. Some call this "Karma;" I call it God's intervention. We can never expect God to make wrongs right at the moment it happens; God's time is much different than our time.

Do you know that even though people don't believe in God they believe in evil? It's true and if you ask those same people why they don't believe in God, they will tell you because they can't see him. If you ask those same people if they believe in evil they will tell you, yes. If you ask the same people why they believe in evil they will tell you that they see evil, in the newspapers and on TV and all around them. Sounds crazy doesn't it? But it is true. So let me help you with this. Everyone believes in the wind! Why? They can't see it. Why then do they believe in the wind? They believe in something they cannot see because they see the **effects** of the wind. They see how the wind blows the leaves of a tree and they **feel** the wind as it blows across their skin. So the only reason they believe in the wind is because they **feel** the **effects** of the wind.

This is the same with the people that say they believe in evil. They believe in evil not because they actually see the evil or the devil (whichever you prefer), but they believe in evil because they see the *effects* of evil and seeing all the evil in the world makes them *feel* a certain way.

When I shared with all of you that I was sexually abused for most of my childhood and that I was also physically abused for most of my childhood, how did that make you *feel*? Did it make you sad, did it hurt your heart inside? Did it bring up a memory of a hardship that you have been through?

Was the answer to both of those questions yes? If so, did you *feel* it inside your heart? If the answer is yes then we are breaking ground here in a powerful way. So if what I just explained is true, the *effects* and *feelings* would be the way we can tell if ANYTHING IS REAL. Whether it is right in front of us, or if it is something we cannot see, *effects* and *feelings* would be our ticket to finding out if something is real or not. How do I know that the love for my wife is real? When I kiss her I *feel* it in my heart and I can see the *effects* of my love for her when she returns the love to me, by a touch or when she says "I love you." I can also tell it is real because of the things she does for me out of love. I know our love is real because of the *effects* and the way it makes me *feel*.

Breaking Chains ~ Paul Aragon

So why do people in recovery find this God? Why do they rely on this God yet they cannot keep themselves clean each day? They do because of the **effects** and **feelings**. They know God is real because they have faith and they trust each day that this infinite God of all power will keep them clean and sober one more day, and everyday they continue to rely on him. *They know God is real because of the effects; that they are clean and sober when years of countless vain attempts brought up nothing until they learned to rely on this power greater than themselves. They also know God is real because of how it makes them feel each day they rely on him. They see the effects of God each day because their attitude and outlook on life is different than before.*

What about the people that get clean and sober without God? Here is where it gets tricky. I have seen many of the people that get clean without an understanding or without a belief in God. Is it possible? Yes it is. But they lack something. I will not discuss that in this book because that is not what this book is for. I do not believe in bashing anyone's recovery. The only thing that I can tell you in this matter is that they lack something.

Why do these people of faith give God all the credit for the work they do? This is another frequently asked question. In our addiction we are very selfish people; everything is about me, me, me, me. Look at me, the center of attention, always controlling conversation and never letting anyone else get a word in edgewise. I was that way too.

We of faith give God the glory because he deserves it. It is a selfless act of gratitude to our God for being in our lives and seeing us through each day. Yes, many addicts in recovery work very hard in their recovery, and its o.k. to acknowledge the hard work you put into your recovery. But once we start telling everyone how hard we worked and how awesome we are, then we are bringing in our recovery what we had in our addiction: *Self-centeredness*.

So we thank God for giving us the strength and the wisdom to make it through each day. In doing so, it begins to set the stage for growth and change that people will see in us even before we see it.

So how do I get to know this God of all understanding? How can I see the *effects* and the *feelings* in my life? The first step is to ask him into your life. Do this in a private place or go visit a pastor at a church and ask him to help you. Pray to him every day to reveal himself to you, and I promise he will!

If the faith you choose is **Bible** based, start reading the Bible every day. I would encourage you to start in the book of John, which will really help you to get to know the Bible based God. Make sure it is a Bible that is easy to read. You can go to any church of faith and get a Bible that is easy to read for free. All you have to do is go in and ask them for a Bible to read.

Bible studies are a very good place to start as well. Every church has one and can easily set you up in a Bible study group. I did this in early recovery to help me learn more, and I did. Also, attending your faith-based church will not only help you get to know God, but you will meet many people there over time. That is always good for recovery because it will enlarge your support system, which is important in recovery.

Remember this in your walk with God. It takes time to get to know people. Actually, when you meet someone it really takes a lifetime to get to know them. Be patient in your walk with God and get to know him over your lifetime. There is no rush. God's not going anywhere.

But meet with him and connect with God every day as you would a friend. Then you will understand that he loves you, and that you are his child and he wants what is best for you. Trust in him. Have faith in him, and you will bear fruit like you never thought you could without him.

Let me share a story of hope with you:

I had been addicted to drugs for 31 years. Many years into my addiction I met the most beautiful woman in the world. She later became my third wife. I had hurt her by my drug addiction terribly. It was never my intention to hurt her, but my drug addiction was my master and it consumed everything in my life.

My wife was a Christian woman who went to church every Sunday. How I landed a woman like her I will never know. I would like to think it was God's intervention. Maybe God wanted to see how much this lady would go through to bring me to him. I don't know. I try not to figure God out; I only strive to know him better every day. She went through so much crap because of me. She was involved in church and read her Bible every day, all while I was out there doing drugs trying to feel normal.

One day, enough was enough. She asked me to leave the home and told me that the marriage was over. I was devastated because this time I knew that she was serious. I knew there was no hope for me coming home again. I was in a sober living home and I was only 24 hours clean and was in full withdrawal. I had just gotten back from my sponsor's house and he didn't want to meet with me because he knew I still had dope in my system. He wanted me clean before we got into the 12 step work, so he told me that he wanted me clean for two weeks and then he would begin the work with me. He said that if I stayed clean for two weeks then that would show him I was serious about recovery.

I lost my wife and I was looking at prison time. All I wanted to do was to get high. I went back to my sober living home and laid my head on my pillow and I began to cry. I cried so hard that I remember lifting up my head and turning my pillow over because it was soaked in tears.

I began to scream at God as I lay there crying. "God, why won't you help me? Why are you putting me through this God?" I said out loud.

I screamed for him to help me. I lay there crying, so sick of my life and lonely for my family. I kept replaying my wife's last words to me in my head, "If you love me you wouldn't keep doing this to me."

As I lay there in the stillness I could hear a soft voice whispering to me. Now this wasn't one of the voices I usually heard when I was high or in withdrawals; this voice was different, more than I had ever heard in my life. It was a soft voice and it relaxed me as it spoke to me. I could feel the voice through my whole body as it spoke to my heart. The voice said to me,

"Paul, you have never given your whole heart to me; I promise you this day, that if you give your whole heart to me and you give your recovery all you have inside you, I will take away your obsession to use drugs."

I knew with all my heart that for the first time in my life, I had just heard God's voice. I believe with all my heart that the only reason I heard God's voice that day was because I was calling to him as I yelled at him in my pillow. I believe that my faith in him was at its highest point in my life up to that point. I was so broken that I turned to God. I really believed in my heart that I was talking to him at that moment, and he responded to my cries.

Do you know how a child cries to their parent when they are unhappy with something in their life? That was how I cried out to God that day.

I have not used drugs since that day, and I have given God all that I have inside me. It has been many, many years since I have used drugs or alcohol of any kind. I have since been reunited with my wife and we have been together for 15 years and are celebrating 10 years of marriage this year. I asked her a few months ago if she would marry me again, and she said yes! This year we will be renewing our vows and this time I will be clean and sober when we do so.

I have been with her more years clean and sober than I was in my addiction and that to me is a success story. It is only by the grace of God that I am here and in this moment. I know I heard his voice that day and it changed my life. I can say to those of you reading this book that if you have tried and tried to get clean and sober and it just hasn't happened yet, you might want to bring God into the picture; and I just don't mean saying it. I mean really bring God into your life, with everything inside you, and I promise you will never do drugs again.

I never dreamed that many years later I would not only have taught recovery all over the United States, but I have even been blessed with teaching Sunday service a few times at my church in the last few years. I will never forget the day God spoke to me.

There is good and there is evil. There is God and there is the devil. They are both fighting to have you. Which one will you serve?

YEA THOUGH I WALK THROUGH THE VALLEY OF THE SHADOW OF DEATH

Yea though I walk through the valley of the shadow of death, I will fear no evil. For God is with me.
The demons they haunt me.
They try to pull me back, into that life.
But with each day I push further and further from my addiction.
I walk through green pastures.
I no longer walk through the desert of darkness.
I have made a choice.
To no longer live in the grip of my addiction.
I know it may follow me.
But I don't look back.
I don't close the door to my past.
For my past will help others like me.
I look at what's in front of me.
God comforts me.
I trust that.
For faith without work is dead faith.
Yea though I walk through the valley of the shadow of death, I will fear no evil.
I know my addiction is always doing push-ups.
Waiting for a moment of weakness in my life.
I too will do spiritual push-ups.
I too will stay spiritually fit.
I will work for each day of freedom that God gives me.
Yea though I walk through the valley of the shadow of death, I will fear no evil.
For the Lord is with me!

Poem by Paul C. Aragon

Chapter 5

Addiction from the Eyes of an Addict

I wish I could tell you that it is just as easy to stop using drugs as it is to start. But it isn't. Drugs have a way of quietly creeping into your life and then taking control of your life like no force on earth. We would love to think that nothing can control our thoughts, our mind and body, but drugs can and will.

But most things we can put a quick stop to, like a bad relationship, a job, or a negative person in our life. Those things can control us for a brief moment but when reality hits, we can easily remove it from our life.

With drugs it isn't that easy. Many people begin using drugs without thought or understanding of what drugs have the potential to do in our life. We start just to be cool with friends or because we have a bad home life, bad parents and even a traumatic situation. These can also be the reasons people pick up and use. Regardless of the reason, addicts never plan on their life spinning out of control and hurting the ones they love in the process.

We said yes when we should have said no; even if we have heard the war stories about drugs and even the warnings that have been laid at our feet at school. It may come as easy as a friend saying; "Trust me you will like it" or "Do you want to try it?" Many are smart or lucky enough to choose friends that are a good influence and they never see the harm drugs really do.

Many start their drug addiction with a hit or two of marijuana, or a cold beer with friends. This cycle may go on for a while. The gentleness and the ease and comfort that come from a simple hit off a pipe go for miles in a chaotic world. Especially for a young person that is so naive to the power and control drugs have over us.

It may take years, but most addicts will see the demons that come with addiction. Whether you are a spiritual, religious person or even an agnostic, every addict may see that there is some sort of bad, evil or demonic force involved when addiction is in its prime. It is a scary and lonely place to be with no way of breaking free from the chains of addiction that bind you.

The cravings that develop in an addict when the addiction cycle takes place is something that you can actually see but have no clue as to why and how to stop it. By the time you see the addiction planting its roots, it's too late. When you take the first hit, almost every addict lifts their hands and says "I am good" after just the first few hits.

In order to understand addiction you must understand the simplicity of how it works and how it takes place in the addict. In order for me to explain that to you I will have to get clinical for a brief moment.

"The "high" that takes place with all drugs happens in the midbrain, AKA the pleasure center of the brain. When we use drugs for the first time, large amounts of chemicals in the brain are released causing the high. When these chemicals are released, "the high" may vary depending upon the type of drug. Drugs trick the brain in different ways to release the chemicals; how the brain receives those chemicals is what causes the high.

The chemicals flood the synapse with a natural chemical in the midbrain called dopamine. This is where the word "dope" comes from. When we have a natural pleasure such as eating, a cell within a cell drops down and releases the dopamine into the synapse where the chemicals are received by neurotransmitters. Then the dopamine travels back to the cell and is taken back into the cell by uptake valves and prepares itself for another pleasure.

When we take a bite of a delicious burger and the smell of it begins to pleasure us, we then begin to salivate; this is the midbrain being pleasured by food.

The brain releases the dopamine in many natural pleasurable ways and depending on what the pleasure is will depend on how much dopamine is released. The largest amount of dopamine released naturally is from sex. So this gives you an idea of how the pleasure center in the brain works. The important thing to know is that drugs don't get you high. The chemicals in the brain are what cause the high.

Each drug releases different amounts of chemicals, which can play a big part in the addiction process. For instance, Methamphetamines are one of the drugs that release the most dopamine at one time. Meth can release approximately 8x more dopamine than sex. So that will give you an idea of how much dopamine is released from drug to drug.

So what causes addiction? When too much dopamine is released, the brain is not used to uptaking that much at one time, so the dopamine gets lost or dissipates in the synapse, meaning it disappears. So the brain has to make more. This is not a quick process. Because the brain doesn't have as much dopamine as the first time you use, the everyday user uses up so much dopamine that the brain can't keep up and it takes more drugs to get the addict high. With drugs like meth and crack cocaine the tolerance level can climb very quickly. When the tolerance level rises, the user begins to become addicted. It is important to know that addiction can be passed down genetically as well. This means that if you have a family member that was addicted to drugs that the chances are good that the sibling may also become addicted more easily if they choose to pick up drugs.

Now that you have a small understanding about addiction we can continue with the addict. Most addicts are normal people, as normal as normal is anyway. They come from all walks of life: rich, poor, middle class, upper class; from bank tellers to construction workers.

No addict grows up saying, "I want to be addicted to drugs when I grow up." Many addicted families have generations of addicts in their family because they do it in front of their kids. You know the saying, "The apple doesn't fall far from the tree." Well, that certainly is usually true when parents do drugs in front of their kids. Many parents think smoking marijuana is o.k. because it is natural; they smoke in their room and try to hide it from the kids. As the kid gets older he realizes mom and dad smoke weed so it must be o.k. Then another addict is born. But this child then takes it to another level and uses harder drugs, and then the parent puts the blame on their kid for making a bad decision to use hard drugs. Ignorant isn't it?

The problem with this is that after a while the marijuana stops working for the user and then they move to a bigger, stronger drug to give them the high they need. Some don't take it to that level, but most do. Many addicts had a good upbringing but the same situation, a bad combination of friends and drugs, and another addict is born.

I remember when I drank my first beer at the age of nine years old. I didn't know what it was or what it would do to me. All I knew is that adults laughed a lot when drinking it; I was going through such a hard childhood that I wanted to feel that way. I remember taking two beers out of my dad's refrigerator in the garage and I went into my closet and I drank both of them as fast as I could. I loved the way it made me feel and the way it made me forget. I fell asleep behind the laundry basket in my closet only to wake up hours later wishing I could drink more. I didn't drink for a few years after that day, but at age 12, I began to drink again. I also started smoking marijuana and I really liked the way it made me feel. I really just wanted anything that would make the pain go away. It wasn't long before I ran away from home and began drinking regularly.

I eventually came off the streets and moved in with my mom for a short period of time. I started drinking her vodka and replacing it with water, she also kept a pretty good supply of beer and I was drinking everyday. She caught onto my vodka trick and I would blame my brother for it but it was me.

I was broken goods and nobody knew it or really seemed to care; so eventually I ran away from home and lived on the streets where I felt at home. By the time I was 15 years old I was an alcoholic and a junkie. It was at that age that I stuck a needle in my arm. I began to rob houses and steal from cars. I even robbed gas station till boxes they kept behind the counter.

I did every drug I could get my hands on and I was high every moment of every day. My tolerance level for drugs seemed to get higher with every passing day. By the time I was sixteen years old I became a black out alcoholic. It wasn't everyday I blacked out, but a few times a week I would black out.

I could tell you that alcohol was my gateway drug, but I really don't believe that to be true. Just because it was the first drug I ever did doesn't necessarily mean that it was my gateway. I believe that marijuana was my gateway drug because of the way it made me feel.

As I explained earlier about how drugs trick the brain into releasing chemicals in the brain that causes the high, alcohol doesn't work like that. So when I used marijuana for the first time and released all those chemicals in the brain, I believe that was when I really fell in love with drugs. It seemed like the more drugs I tried the better it got for me. I had no interest in high school or anything else but getting high. I had nobody to tell me what to do or even to help me if I needed help. I was on my own.

I don't even think I ever felt withdrawals of any kind until I was in my later teens because I was always high. I started selling drugs at sixteen years old to supply my addiction. I had every drug I knew of on me for sale. I was a walking drug store.

I am sharing my childhood with you because I want you to see how quickly addiction can take place and how quickly it can ruin your life. I didn't know better. I didn't have a mom or dad who cared enough to fight for me. I was lost from the moment I was born into a broken family, to a neighbor that would rape me over and over again for many years, until I was old enough to run away from home and never return. My mom and dad divorced when I was three and that devastated me. I had no one to protect me and no one to love me. I was doomed to be addicted.

So when I hear people make stupid comments like, "Why do drug addicts even pick up in the first place?" or "It's their own fault for making bad choices," it upsets me. People can be so naive just because it didn't happen to them. They got it all figured out. Many addicts have been through some pretty horrific things as a child. Others make bad choices with no parental guidance. Others are just rebellious and parents feel like they are at a loss and they're not, they just choose to be. Let the kid run away, don't look for him just let him go and you end up with an addict like me.

I don't think anyone should judge an addict before knowing their story. Every addict is someone's child regardless of why they picked up. Every addict is a child of God and should be treated as such. Be careful if you judge others because that is how you will be judged. I believe that to be true. We should spend more time trying to reach out to those who want to be reached out to, instead of pushing them away because it's something you don't understand.

Addiction can be scary if you don't understand it, so get to know it and understand it. Then you can combat it whether you're an addict or the loved one of an addict.

Breaking Chains: Chronicles of a Meth Addict

I look back,
I will never forget the pain,
It was hard,
Like Breaking Chains.
They held me so tight,
Wrapped around me,
Now I am becoming all I can be.
My life was like hiding in an attic,
These are the Chronicles of a Meth Addict.
On the streets, pain and misery,
I couldn't go home,
I was ashamed for my family to see me.
The remorse always came,
And it was like hell,
There I sat in another jail cell.
Tears would fall down like rain,
Will I ever Break these Chains?
My life was like a tornado,
Never knowing which way to go.
My thinking was always so static,
These are the Chronicles of a Meth Addict.
All the people who wanted to believe in me,
Wasn't enough for my recovery.
The thought of using would always torment me,
It was like a demon living inside me.

Breaking Chains ~ Paul Aragon

The justification, and rationalization,
Only fed my frustration.
The people I have hurt,
It's hard to break free
From the chains that bind me.
But now I am clean,
And my life is serene.
Sometimes it feels like a dream.
I reach out to others,
People like me.
It reminds me of what I used to be.
Sometimes I feel so sporadic,
These are the Chronicles of a Meth Addict.

Poem by Paul C. Aragon

Chapter 6

Depression in Recovery

This chapter is devoted to those that suffer from addiction in recovery. This chapter is written from my own experience, and not from a clinical point of view, for which I am not qualified. I will share my story with you and the things that worked for me in my battle with addiction.

My story begins when I had about three and a half years clean and sober. I was very involved in my recovery, going to school to be a counselor, volunteering in A.A. (Alcoholics Anonymous), involved in many ministries at my church, and leading Celebrate Recovery groups. I also was sponsoring several men in the 12 steps. My recovery was through the roof, and outside of work, I was busy for the majority of the remaining hours of my day.

Recovery can be tough, especially when you have a family that suffered at the hands of your addiction. Learning how to be a parent and a husband was not even on the radar because I thought that being clean and sober was enough. I thought I was going over and above what most people do in their recovery, and I did. But my marriage was failing and we were in constant fights about how I treated her and the kids. I assumed my wife was just picking on me. How could she think this way? Wasn't it enough that I was clean and sober and helping others? I really thought she was being ridiculous. But was she? No, she wasn't. She wanted a husband and dad. I didn't know how to be one, so I drowned myself in my recovery ignoring her pleas.

Through my earlier years in recovery I had bouts of depression, but they were small and through God I managed to work my way through them. My wife and I were arguing all the time and it got to a point that my wife wanted out of the marriage; but she kept hanging on to the hope that I would see her concerns as a parent. She was hoping for her husband to be the dad and the husband that she knew I could be. It wasn't that I was a bad parent as much as it was that I just didn't know how to parent or be a husband.

The depression began to show its head during this time. We had little money and I had lost my job on top of the craziness of a failing marriage. My wife tried to help me, even through all the anger and resentment she had towards me at the time. Back and forth trips to the doctor to try to get my depression medication leveled out to where it should be didn't seem to help. My depression was getting worse by the day.

I got a phone call one day from my brother and he told me something that was hard for me to swallow. My mother was on life support and was dying. The doctor wanted to give family members the time to come and say their goodbyes before taking her off life support. So I jumped in my truck and took off across the states to say goodbye to my dear mom.

When I got to the hospital my brother was there but the rest of my brothers and sisters couldn't make it. When they took her off life support, I heard my mom take the most horrific breath of air I had ever heard in my life. I began to cry. My oldest brother and I prayed for her, and then my brother had to leave. He couldn't watch my mother pass. He didn't want to remember t her that way. I couldn't blame him. But I felt as the youngest son and all my years in addiction that I owed it to my mom to be there for her and guide her into God's hands. I was alone. I sang worship songs to my mother as she lay there helpless and in pain. I prayed for her countless times and even took out my Bible and read her verses from God's word.

My mom would wake up when the morphine wore off. I would have to call the nurse in to give her more, and as she grew silent again from the morphine, I was left listening to her labored breathing. It was the hardest thing I have ever been through in my life. The hospital gave me her meals and they even made a bed for me next to my mom because I told them I wasn't leaving my mother's side. I wanted to be there when she left this world and when God was ready to receive this unbelievable woman of faith to our Lord and Savior.

Days passed and my mother was still hanging on. I couldn't understand why she wouldn't let go. When the morphine wore off, my mother would wake. She was coherent and knew that it was me by her side. I would speak to her and she would talk with me, but she was in pain. Again, I would have to call the nurse in to give her more morphine. I remember asking her once when she was awake, "Mom, why won't you let go?" It was the one question she didn't answer. So I got this thought that she was waiting for my brothers and sisters to show up. So the next time she woke up, I called my brothers and sisters and let them say goodbye. I could hear my brothers and sisters talking to my mom and I heard her say the same thing to each of them in a laboring voice: "I love you too, honey," she said. I didn't want to overwhelm my mom with too many phone calls because she was in a lot of pain. So I would do two phone calls every time she woke up.

After almost a full day, I got through all my brothers and sisters; they all said their goodbyes. It took five days and four nights for my mom to pass from the time they took her off life support. It was the most horrifying five days of my life. I watched her turn from a grape to a raisin in just a few days. The memory still haunts me. Two hours after my mom said goodbye to my last sibling, she passed. I heard her take a huge breath as I held her hand and I watched the pulse on her neck beat for the last time. I climbed up on the bed and lay next to her as her body grew cold.

Her son who had finally found his way to a clean and sober life had been there by her side. I was proud of myself, and my brothers and sisters were so proud of me as well.

The long drive home to another state seemed to take forever. I was in deep thought of what had happened the past five days. It was embedded in my heart and in my head. Never once did I think of using drugs. It wasn't even a thought.

When I got home my wife tried to be as supportive as I would allow her to be, but I withdrew into my own shell of anger. My marriage was still falling apart. The medication didn't seem to help me and thoughts of suicide were pounding in my brain. I wanted to tell my wife, but we were not doing well at all. I tried to fight off the thoughts as best I could.

Three weeks after my mother passed, I ended up in a parking lot and slit my wrist. I think I was just crying for help from someone, anyone. I called 911 as blood dripped from my wrist, and six police cars surrounded my truck with guns drawn. They asked me to get out of the truck with my hands in the air. I stepped out of my truck with my keys and my cell phone.

Then they asked me to drop everything I had on the ground. I told them I had to call my wife. So I called my wife and told her where I was and what had happened. My wife didn't take it well. I think it scared the hell out of her.

The police put me in back of the car and off to the psych ward I went. They kept me over the 72 hour hold on a 5150 (California code which allows a qualified clinician to confine a person if they are a danger to themselves or others) because my wife would not allow me to come home. I sent her over the top and my marriage was over. How could this happen? I wasn't even doing drugs and I still managed to lose my family again. I sunk deeper into my depression. They wouldn't release me from the 5150 hold because I had nowhere to go.

The pastor at my church managed to get a hold of the sober living home where I got clean and sober before, and they allowed me to come back with open arms. Back in a recovery home with three and a half years clean and sober was tough; I fought my pride on that one, and really had to practice humility.

My wife was kind and she was sweet to me, but she set her boundaries in place and it was clear that the marriage was over. I didn't understand at the time why she left me, but I clearly understand now. The most important things in my life were God and my family, and I had let one of them down. I believe to this day that nothing in God's world happens by mistake. This was just going to be another chapter in my life and recovery because I had made it through all that without ever a thought of using drugs. I was too far in my recovery for that to even be a thought.

In that recovery home I would always start my day with prayer and meditation as I did even when I was at home with my family. I was missing something back when I was with my family, and I was about to learn what that something was.

I was on the back patio of the recovery home one morning. The sun was barely coming up over the horizon. I prayed and sat there in the quietness of the still morning. The birds were just starting to wake up as I began hearing their voices sing in the soft morning air.

I heard a quiet voice speak to me. I heard this voice before when I first got clean and sober. I knew it was God talking to my broken heart. I have had many people ask me what God's voice sounds like when he talks to us. The only way for me to explain it is that it is like having a conversation with one's self. The only difference is that I am never as smart as God and that is how I know in my heart that it wasn't me. God has a very soft voice and there is no real tone like in our voice; it's a very faint whisper that is felt in the heart and received in the heart.

That morning God spoke to my heart and he said to me, "Paul, would you give up your family for me?" I answered back to him with my inside voice, "Yes father, I would give up my family for you." Well that was a no brainer. I had already lost my family, so that was an easy yes.

Then I heard God's voice again, "Paul, would you give up your family for me?" "Yes, I would give up my family for you father," I replied. This time I said it out loud.

Four hours later I went to my wife's house to pick up some of my DVD's. When I got there I said hello to my kids. It was so nice to feel them in my arms. I thought of them every moment. I gathered up my DVD's after visiting with then and my wife asked if she could talk to me for a moment. I set the DVD's down and went and sat down at the table where she was sitting. "What's up?" I asked. My wife then proceeded to tell me that her mom suggested that she and the kids come and stay with them in Oregon for a while and that she would return to California in a year. "I can't take the kids without your consent," she said.

"You're not coming back here if you leave, who you are trying to kid? No, you're not taking my kids out of this state," I replied.
Just then I heard God's voice again, just like I did four hours earlier.

"Paul, I thought you said you would give your family up for me," God said.

"Are you serious?" I thought. "This can't be happening to me!"

I knew it was God's voice. So I stood up from the table, after hearing God's reminder, and told her, "Go. You have my permission." I quickly left the house in tears, feeling as though I had just signed my kids away. But I had no doubt that it was God's voice, and that he wanted to meet me in a personal and private place. He had something in store for me.

I drove down the street in tears and I didn't get but a block away and my wife had called me on my cell phone. "What happened?" she asked. My wife is a good Christian woman and she knew that something more happened to me than just me saying yes. I told her about my conversation with God hours earlier and she knew God wanted to meet me alone with no interruptions.

Now my depression jumped to a higher level. Watching my wife pack up the house and preparing to leave me behind. I told her before she left that I was going to save my money and that I would be there in a year that I wasn't going to be a dad from a state away. Then they were gone.

I had to address this depression. My kids were gone and my wife, whom I loved, was gone. Everyone blamed me for her leaving. Perhaps they were right. I did everything I could to keep from picking up that knife again.

So I fought for my life. I needed to find out what it was that God wanted for me and my life. I got busy into Bible studies and took a few parenting classes. I even went to a marriage class through the church. I was the only man there without a wife by his side. I absorbed all that I could. I read the whole bible in a year and God even showed me why he wanted me alone for that year. God wanted me to learn how to be a husband and father. He also wanted to teach me how to handle my depression on my own. I went to counseling with three different pastors during that year and really worked on some things that were an easy fix for me.

I had to realize that I was being selfish in my marriage and that I didn't use what I had learned in recovery with my wife. I needed to be a good listener and set boundaries; not only in my recovery but with my family too, and I didn't do that. The depression took roots to the frustration of my own doing.

Breaking Chains ~ Paul Aragon

I also had to deal with the fact that I was raped and beat as a child. That took its toll on me and was never really addressed in my recovery.

I have learned so much through the years about depression and how the brain suffers when the drugs are removed. Depression can last for many years and it can come and go without warning. Having the proper tools to deal with depression when it does creep into your life is paramount. I am a firm believer in therapy and how it can help someone with depression.

Depression is also caused by drug use and is part of PAWS (Post Acute Withdrawals Syndrome). I will talk more about that in the chapter titled "Withdrawals from Drugs."

I also believe that if someone has a good doctor who can monitor them closely, there are some good medications which can help with depression. Medications aren't for me because I have learned to use my tools and learned how to retrain my brain to think differently when the storms in my life arise. Not everyone can do this, but everyone has the ability to do this. It is always important to have a person to call and talk to when you are depressed. Many people believe it is wrong to be depressed and that they shouldn't feel this way, so they hold it inside like I did for so long. When a person does this, the depression will worsen. Don't be afraid to talk to your pastor, a therapist or a very close friend when depression is evident. Believe it or not, exercise can also help with depression because it releases "happy" endorphins in the brain. I have found that a simple hobby like art, painting, crocheting, sculpting, drawing, etc., can really help when your mind won't stop screaming.

Using your tools may work for one person and not for another. This is why it is important to try different things that can work for you. Taking long walks can also help to relieve depression. Recovery from depression is not an overnight matter. It can take a long time to get past, but with work and consistency you can get through and past depression.

Many people sit in a pool of depression, and it only gets worse. I have found with depression that it's best talking about what is causing the depression with another person. Try to pinpoint what is causing you to be depressed. A therapist is trained to do just that. They can go back into your past and pinpoint one or many things that are causing the depression. Once you find out why you're depressed, the rest can be down hill from there. The toughest part of depression is finding out the reason or reasons you are depressed. I have heard many people say that they don't know why they are depressed; they just are. You are not alone. Many people do not know why they are depressed, and that is best left up to a professional.

Once you figure out why you are depressed it is only half the battle. Then you should address the issue with consistency, work and understanding as to why you are depressed. Many addicts in recovery suffer because of the brain putting itself back together from the damage done. There may be more there than just the damage to the brain. The depression may also stem from something that happened in your past that went years without being detected. Drugs are a master at hiding our feelings and emotions. Then when we get clean and sober the emotions come out and it has been so many years since the cause of the depression that you may not even have an idea as to why you are depressed.

When I told you the story above and my wife moved to Oregon I addressed my depression for the year that she was gone and was able to work through depressed times. When I got to Oregon, I lived alone without my family or friends. I didn't know anyone. I was in a foreign land.

Breaking Chains ~ Paul Aragon

At that time, I felt my depression coming back. So I went to a hobby store and bought a 36x20 inch canvas and some paints and I began to paint. I had never painted a canvas before and I always wanted to. I was always good at drawing but never did a canvas. I began to free hand this huge canvas and the result took me straight out of my depression. Not only because it took weeks to complete but because it was beautiful when I completed it. It lifted my spirits to a whole new level.

I painted (freehand) a picture of Jesus walking on water in the stormy sea. His hand was reaching out to the person looking at the painting and the hand of Jesus was in 3D. I didn't plan it that way but it came out that way. Jesus was reaching out to me in the painting. My wife and I got back together years ago and we are doing so well. My kids are a joy and I have become the husband and father that I always knew I could be. Getting past the depression was the key. Achieving that with the family gone was so crucial in my recovery from depression.

That was a very uncomfortable moment for me; giving up my family. Remember I told you earlier in the book, that if it is uncomfortable then you probably need to do it? Well you need to do it because it will bring about change. It brought change to me. It was hard, but it was well worth it.

It has been many years now since depression has showed its ugly head in me. It may again one day, but I have the tools to keep it at bay when and if it does.

Knowing where depression comes from and why it's there are key factors when combatting depression. The brain suffers at the hand of addiction. I have found that drugs like methamphetamines cause so much damage to the brain that the brain can take a long time putting itself back together. In that process is where the depression comes from. Retraining your brain to think differently takes consistency and time. A person that sits around all day long and does nothing to address their depression is more likely to have a fall out. How we respond to situations and tough times in our life can limit how much depression affects us. Therapists are very good at teaching these skills.

Many people will tell you that if you are a person of faith that you just need to trust God and let him heal you through faith. I am not going to tell you that these people are wrong, but I will tell you that God has blessed people with many gifts. Doesn't his word tell us this? God has blessed us with therapists, doctors and even medication to help us heal in different ways. Do what is best for you and use the tools that I have given you. Can God ultimately heal you? Yes, but I believe that he has put people in our lives to help us; and there is a little more to it than just doing nothing.

I can also tell you that there are a lot of natural and healthy ways to combat depression using natural herbs, plants and foods. If you're not a fan of doctors and prescribed medications, then go online and educate yourself on some of the natural ways people combat depression.

The important thing is to do what is comfortable and what works for you. If it doesn't work then try something else. The most important thing is eat right and stay busy.

People of faith also believe that depression is just Satan, and that you just need to ignore him. Does the devil have a hand in depression? Satan's hand is in everything that hinders us. Is it all Satan's fault? Sure, if you want to blame the drugs on him. I know what happens in the brain when coming off drugs. The chemicals are so out of whack, that when you remove that drug and the brain is no longer getting those surges of chemicals, it is thrown into turmoil. The brain is great at repairing itself and it can take up to 18 months for the brain to get the chemical balance as close as possible to normal. Will the brain fix itself completely? Not necessarily. It all depends on how much damage you have done and that is determined by how long you have used, how often you used, your tolerance level, and size and weight. Everyone is different.

If you use the tools that are suggested by your therapist, pastor, or doctor then you have the opportunity to heal. Reading my Bible daily on a consistent basis helped me because it gave me something that my spirit needed and it took my mind off of the things that weighed on me. I believe a positive book can do this as well, I just chose the bible. God does take part in the healing process, but there is always work you have to do in order for God to begin his work in you.

I will end with this short story: There was a man drowning in the ocean. He shouted out to God, "God please help me!" Just then an ocean liner came by and threw the man a life preserver. The man shouted back, "It's ok, God is going to save me!" The man surely had faith and trusted in God. Just then a sailboat came by and threw the man a life preserver. The man shouted, "It's ok, God is going to save me!" The man surely had faith and trusted in God. Just then a helicopter came overhead and threw the man a life preserver. The man shouted back, "It's ok, God is going to save me." The man surely had faith and trusted in God. A short time later the man drowned in the ocean. The man went to heaven and when he got there he asked God, "Lord, I prayed to you, I asked you to help me Lord." To which the Lord replied, "My child I tried to save you three times and you ignored me all three times."

Just because you have trust and faith does not mean that you don't use the people that God puts in your life to help you. How can God help you if you refuse his help? Faith without works is dead faith. God puts people, pastors, doctors, counselors, therapists, psychologists, mentors, and sponsors in our life so we can use them to get through the rough spots. God uses other people to bless and guide us. I will say it one more time in closing: ***Faith without works is dead faith!!***

NEVER GIVE UP

I needed healing,
From the way,
That I was feeling.
I was on my knees,

I was crying inside,
I was dying inside,
Nobody could hear my screams.
I want it just to leave me,
The darkness inside me,
How can this happen to me,
Without the dope inside me,
It's still haunting me,
And it's not in my veins no more,
God can you save me?
I am crying all the time,
I am hiding all the time,
I don't want anyone around me,
I don't do dope anymore.
And I still feel like it is robbing me,
Of my sanity,
Where is my joy?
Please save me God,
From what's inside me,
I am waiting for a hero,
That hero is Lord,
I'm never going back,
To the dope,
That caused this pain,
I've got to stand up,
And make another change,
I did it before,
I can do it again,
Because I believe in me.

By Paul C. Aragon

Chapter 7

Sexual Addictions

I know many people reading this book are wondering why there is a chapter about sexual addictions in a book about drug addiction. I am also sure there are others saying they are so glad there is a chapter about sexual addiction in this book. By the time I am through with this chapter, you will know why this chapter is here

Believe it or not, sexual addiction is probably the biggest addiction on earth. More people than you can possibly imagine suffer at the hand of the addiction to sex regardless of the form. There is no way to tell the percentages of families that have been torn apart due to sex and the addiction to sex, but I can tell you that it is higher than you might realize.

Sex addiction is one of those things that most people don't talk about, especially spouses who suffer at the hand of sex addiction with a loved one who is addicted to sex.

Sex addiction can come in many forms, from thoughts of sexual acts with another person, to masturbation, sex with prostitutes, promiscuous sex, pornography, porn sites on the internet, sexual chat rooms, sexting (sex talk or inappropriate talk via texting), phone sex, and porn magazines.

Many couples addicted to sex can partake in all of these and never even know that it is a problem in their life, just like a couple addicted to drugs. Many couples watch porn together, with friends and even share partners. Like alcohol, sex is socially acceptable, and it may go unnoticed in a relationship for a long period of time.

Like drugs, sex tolerance level rises. This means that the sex addict feels the need for more and more to satisfy the heightened chemical release. Sex is a natural pleasure given to us, so when we are having sex or masturbating, the same area of the brain is affected similar to drugs but in a natural way. During sex with a spouse chemicals in the brain are released in the midbrain, the same place that drugs take control of. So chemicals are released in small amounts during foreplay all the way up to climax where the largest natural amounts of feel good chemicals are released. This is the highest natural release of chemicals produced from the brain at one time.

There are approximately 200ng of chemicals released at one time during climax or orgasm, which could be one of the scientific reasons as to why addiction takes place in the brain with sex.

Let's face it, drugs aren't the only addiction. There is sex addiction, food addiction, video game addiction, internet addiction, shopping addiction, gambling addiction, shoes addiction, material addiction, codependency addiction, addiction to money; you get the point right? There are so many addictions in this world that I would need a few pages to write them all. Just because you're addicted to sex is no reason to put your head down in shame and crawl in a corner and cry. But like all the addictions I have just mentioned it needs to be addressed. Sex addiction can cause heartache to families just like drugs. For instance, a spouse might feel rejected because you want to watch porn rather than having sex with them.

Sex outside the marriage is not ok, not just for what it does to your spouse and family but also because of what it does to you, inside as a person. Unhealthy sex acts can change who you are inside. It can make you bitter, angry, defensive all the time, cause mood swings, and can bring your spirit down. What I mean by that is that it can steal your joy from you. Yes, sex is a pleasure that we all were gifted to enjoy but it can also be a burden when we use it in a fashion that wasn't intended for us.

For me, sex is a gift that God gave us to enjoy with a spouse. I believe in my heart that all natural pleasures are God given but they all can be misused. So, do you want to hear my own personal definition of what addiction is? My definition of addiction is *anything that we do over and over again without God.* That's pretty deep isn't it? If that is true, this world is in trouble, and it is!

I actually think addictions can be helpful when we look past all the damage addiction can cause. Addiction is can be helpful, for some people who would never seek opportunity to change. People who make a conscious choice to change their life after addiction can become the finest people I have ever known.

Breaking Chains ~ Paul Aragon

The reason is that they change who they are from the inside out. For instance, I wouldn't be here writing this book to help people had I never started drugs. Because of my addiction, I have not only sponsored hundreds of men in recovery but I have also reached out to thousands of people across the world through my web page. That doesn't even include what this book may do, and the people I will continue to reach, all because of my addiction.

If you recognize that you have an addiction and you address the addiction and move away from it, it can make you a better person inside. It can actually help you to be able to help others like you. This is a selfish world with or without addictions. It just seems like people with addiction issues are more selfish than the people without addiction issues. It becomes their sole purpose to fulfill that addiction without the thought of hurting others in the process. The addiction becomes first and foremost in the life of an addict, regardless of the addiction.

Sex addiction is not an issue that people want to talk about openly because it is private and can be embarrassing. It is easy to talk to other addicts about drugs because they relate to you and it isn't as private as sex. But talking about sex in a room full of other people with sexual addictions can be uncomfortable, even if it is talked about with people of the same sex. So people avoid it, say they won't do it or don't need it.

But like 12 step drug and alcohol programs, sexual addiction groups with people of the same sex can be very helpful in a way to let you know that you are not alone. You find a sponsor just like other 12 step groups with a person that has clean time away from their sexual addiction to take you through the 12 steps. The groups are run the same way as drug and alcohol groups. I would encourage you find one that isn't set up for both sexes. I would suggest you find one that is set up with the same sex so you can freely talk about your struggles with others in open forum. There are many churches that offer this and separate the men and women.

Many people in recovery bring sex addiction into their recovery because many drugs alter an addict's sex drive, and open or promiscuous sex was practiced in their addiction. The addict works on the drug addiction and ignores the sexual addiction and it ends up becoming a problem causing just as much damage to their family than drugs, sometimes even more.

When I got clean and sober, I brought my sex addiction into my marriage. It caused so much damage in my marriage that at times I thought I would never be able to repair the damage.

Even though I was just watching porn, to a spouse it's just like cheating on them. What happens is the spouse will cut you off from having sex with them yet the desire for sex is still there, and it can drive you further into your addiction. The dishonesty and the sneakiness are equal to drug addiction. Now your spouse is not giving you attention because they are hurt. Can you blame them? Of course you can't. They feel as if you cheated on them and in a sense you did.

So now you're not getting the attention from your spouse or mate, and you're not getting sex so you look for the attention elsewhere. So what the addict will do is flirt with people online, with texting or even at recovery meeting to fulfill their desire for attention sexually. This eventually causes more problems for the addict and spouse because like drugs they eventually catch you in the act. They will find text messages, check your email account, and find porn magazines in your car or DVD's hidden around the house.

So how does an addict stop this crazy cycle that can destroy the relationship and still get what they need? To be honest, you're going to have to go without your need for sex and attention. It's just like a drug. You have to remove it from your life until you can repair the relationship in a healthy way. When the spouse is ready, you can slowly bring the intimacy back in your life in a healthy way. Just like with drugs, you have to bring the trust back in your relationship. The best way is to stay away from the sexual triggers.

When I was ready to remove my sex addiction from my life I signed up and went to 12 step sex addiction groups and began to learn ways to talk to my spouse about how I was feeling and when I was having urges. I also gave her the time she needed to begin to trust me again.

I stayed away from the internet for months just so she could see me trying. Believe it or not, it took years for me to avoid the things that triggered me. I am not proud of it and it is hard for me to talk about it here for the world to see.

Eventually, when I worked on my sex addiction as hard as I worked on my drug addiction, I began to make progress. After time my wife began to see that I was trying to move away from that part of my life and love her the way she deserved to be loved by her husband. I will not engage in sexual talk with another person or on the internet because I don't want to hurt my wife that way anymore simply because I love her.

Eventually our intimacy returned and was even better than it was before because she knew how hard I worked to show her how much I love her.

I remember her telling me once that it hurt her worse than my drug addiction did. When she found out I was flirting on the internet or was on porn sites it would crush her. It makes the other person feel that they are not attractive or that you're not attracted to them. It lowers their self esteem and makes them feel that they just aren't good enough. This can cause a whole slew of problems for them as well.

My wife and I went to a lot of marriage counseling to heal our marriage. Seeing a marriage counselor can be very helpful if you're honest about yourself. There were many times that I wasn't honest in the counselor's office and it didn't help the situation at all. But when I finally decided to get honest and take accountability for my actions then the healing process was able to take place.

When I was in early recovery I always went to my wife and would talk to her when I was having cravings and she would help me through it in some way. This needs to happen with sex addiction as well. The spouse can't get upset because the addict came to them and shared that he was triggered by a commercial on TV. You should be able to talk to each other openly in order to heal together.

This is why a sexual addiction sponsor and the 12 steps can help you to quickly move through the process rather than trying to do it on your own. It will also show your spouse that you acknowledge you have a problem and that you love them enough to try and fix it.

Sometimes just stopping the act isn't enough. It takes work to learn how to cope with your addiction and how to put tools in place to learn how to maintain long term recovery from your sexual addictions. Like drug addiction, it is a lifelong journey to continue to move away from your addiction.

Many people ask me what to do when there is cheating involved. I personally don't like to see any marriage dissolve for any reason. But if you fix the issues before they can cause permanent damage to your relationship or marriage, then I believe it can be repaired and can eventually be better than before. It is a very hard thing to deal with when a spouse knows you have been with another person sexually, and this can takes years to repair.

Can it be repaired or is it a loss? I know that with God all things are possible if both parties are willing to do what it takes to repair the damage done. But just saying that you will never do it again is not enough to grow and move past the damage you have created. It takes work and willingness to do what it takes to show your spouse that you are willing to address your addiction.

Are all people who cheat addicts? No, many are either just selfish desires or a deeper issue within the marriage itself. Either way there is no justifiable reason to cheat on the one you love.

Let's face it; some people don't have it in their hearts to forgive their spouse for cheating because it is a personal and private act that belongs to the one you married. Sex addiction causes damage whether you are single or in a relationship because it drains your spirit. It doesn't do it exactly the way drugs do, but it is very similar.

Lastly, don't be afraid to address your sex addiction and try to do it before it manifests itself into something that makes it harder to break free from. A pastor from your church, marriage counselors, 12 step sexual addiction groups, and sexual addiction counselors are a great place to start to address you addiction. Most importantly, you have to be honest with yourself that there is a problem.

Inward Reflections

Am I nothing?
To seek the pleasures of an outwardly world?
I was lost for so many years.
That this new life is blind to me.
I seek a generic love.
From a touch that seems to sooth me.
It has overtaken me.
Now it seems to be a need within me.
I feel dirty.
Have I traded one addiction for another addiction?
I must break free from the lies,
My heart is telling me.
Those that submit to me desires,
Are they not sick too?
My heart tells me my body is a temple.
And should be treated as such.
I am worth so much more than this generic pleasure,
that is meant for a man and woman, In holy matrimony.
I should not be concerned with outward beauty.

Breaking Chains ~ Paul Aragon

Rather than with inward reflections
I want that.
I want to save my heart for God's intentions for me.
I want to heal.
I don't want to feel dirty.
I want to feel real love.
I will cleanse my soul in repentance.
I will be healed.
I will wash away my desires of the mind, and seek the
desires of my heart.
Those desires...
are not of this world.

By Paul C. Aragon

Chapter 8

Withdrawal from Drugs

In order to understand withdrawals, it is important to understand what withdrawals are. Withdrawals are symptoms that occur when discontinuing or decreasing the use of drugs, whether it is recreational drugs or abused prescribed medications. It's how the body reacts when the drugs are taken away from the body and the brain as well.

Many of the symptoms you will see in the withdrawal stages include nightmares, vomiting, irritability, fatigue, shaking, sweating, nausea, insomnia, headaches, and altered mood swings. With methamphetamines you may also see flu like symptoms.

Taking drugs, like opiates and benzodiazepines, away from the body abruptly can be fatal. In cases like this, it is best to go to an inpatient facility that specializes in drug detox, to safely remove the drug without harm to the body.

Withdrawal symptoms can be evident in addicts that aren't seeking recovery; they can and will show when time passes without the drug in their system. During this stage, mood swings are altered. Many addicts heavy in their addiction will do anything to avoid withdrawals, such as steal money from a loved one or steal material things that they can trade for the drug.

How long withdrawals last really depends on the drug and the tolerance level of the addict. But in most cases the withdrawal can last on the average of five days into a few weeks. During this time, when an addict chooses to get clean and sober, it is important to rest for a three day period. It is also important that the addict drink lots of fluids to help the drug pass through the body quickly. Fruits are the best way I have found to help with cleaning the body out from drugs in a healthy way. So eat lots of fruit and take multivitamins to help restore the body's nutrients in a safe way. It is also important to start healthier eating habits immediately and at set times during the day.

Breakfast, lunch and dinner should be as close to the same time every day so the body can begin to learn to function properly again. Addicts typically have bad eating habits that can throw the digestive track out of whack and cause more complicated medical issues. So it is important to give the body what it needs when it needs it, starting with the basic food groups.

It is also important to get the addict up after three days, get them mobile and moving around and begin their life of recovery. When an addict stays in bed for long periods of time this will affect the recovery process and can spiral the addict into the stages of depression.

When the body is idle, even just in a sitting position, the body won't produce the chemicals or nutrients that give us motivation and energy. When this happens for prolonged periods of time, the addict will play that tape in their head that drugs are the only way to get them out of bed or off the couch.

This is why recovery programs are effective in the process of recovery because it helps an addict to build a strong support system and gives them a strong foundation to a new life of recovery.

Many addicts won't even try to go to a meeting out of sheer laziness. They think they can recover on their own and without help, and the percentile of those that do is very low.

After the withdrawals, many addicts will go through what is known in the substance abuse field, as ***Post Acute Withdrawal Syndrome*** or **PAWS.** PAWS may start after (post) the withdrawals and are symptoms that the addict goes through without the drugs in their system.

These are a few of the symptoms you may see while in the PAWS stage: Anhedonia (inability to feel natural pleasures in the things that once pleasured you), depression (this is very common in PAWS in most users), obsessive compulsive disorder or OCD, cravings for more drugs, memory problems, sleep disturbances, panic disorder, laziness, anxiety disorder, pessimistic thoughts, suicidal thoughts, and psychosocial dysfunctions.

Some of the symptoms of PAWS may last weeks, months and even years. But don't let this keep you from recovery. Many addicts get past this quickly if they STAY BUSY in their recovery and putting their life back on track.

The people I see that suffer from PAWS the longest and hardest are those who lie in bed all day or sit on the couch doing nothing and calling that recovery. That is not recovery. Recovery is working some type of program that changes who you are from the inside out. If you are removing the drug what do you have? What you have is an addict without the drug.

We did this in our addiction when the dope man was out of dope. Why then would we do this in trying to get off drugs and call it recovery? It is the furthest thing from recovery.

Recovery is when we work on our life, put it back together, stop our selfish motives, and we begin to feel emotions we never felt before. We make new clean and sober friends, get a job and change our life. We in recovery move as far away from our old life as possible. That's recovery.

Addicts have feelings. They love, they hurt, they can sometimes cry, unless they have taught themselves to keep the tears turned off. But even with the tears off, they feel remorse. They also feel guilt and sorrow. Drugs have the power to mask the pain in addicts. When an addict is in withdrawals or coming down, the real person will try to emerge, and all those feelings I just mentioned will be amplified. Some addicts (very few) have learned to shut that off because of the pain and sorrow they go through. None that I have seen are able to hide the depression that follows from the lack of drugs in their system.

Yes, we cause pain. Yes, we make bad choices. If you have never been an addict, you will never understand what it is an addict goes through. We addicts make the bad choice to use drugs, but we don't choose addiction, addiction chooses us.

Most people that use drugs for the very first time really don't understand what addiction really is, and others think that will never happen to them. Addicts essentially use because of the ease and comfort it gives them regardless of the drug or the high.

I guess the part that most people just can't understand is why an addict would give up their kids, put their kids in harm's way, lose their families, and lose their spouses after many begs and pleas to stop. Loved ones will give everything they have for their loved one on dope. They do not listen to anyone that says anything negative about them and they will help them at all cost. Yet the addict will beg, borrow, steal and sell everything they own for a quick fix. We as addicts don't set out to have our kids taken away, nor do we wish to lose a loved one to drugs. But that craving inside our body for more is so intense that we have to feed it. It is a pain that all addicts bear. If it were easy, more addicts would be getting clean. Drugs affect the brain in such a way that we have taught the brain to depend on them. By stopping abruptly we will and do suffer our consequences for saying yes the very first time. Most heavy addicts wish they could start all over and go back to that first yes, and say no. We have dreams that have been destroyed by dope and it kills us inside as the years pass as we watched our life pass by.

The first thing you need to learn about addiction is that each addict is different. The recovery process may be different. The choice of drugs may be different, and the way that drug affects them, may be different as well. There are so many things that come into play when we talk about drugs and how bad an addict really is.

One of the most frequent questions I get asked is: Is my loved one an addict? Addicts will also ask me: How do I know I am an addict? Some addicts will be in denial about their addiction and many make statements like "I don't have a problem."

The simplest way to find out if you or your loved one is an addict is by withdrawals. Withdrawal syndrome is what happens when the drug is taken from the body. It's how the body reacts when the drug is taken away. If the withdrawals take place, then the chances are pretty good that you or your loved one is dependent on that drug. This means that you have used this drug enough to where the body craves it and the brain has been taught to need it.

Some drugs cause emotional withdrawals and physical withdrawals, whereas other drugs may just cause emotional withdrawals. Some create both. Different drugs can cause more of one and less of the other depending on the drug and the tolerance level of the addict.

The symptoms of emotional withdrawals are depression, headaches, low concentration, insomnia, isolation, irritability, and restlessness. Depression should be expected with most drugs because of everything that is involved when taking the drug away to how the addict feels about the choices they made to use. Depression may also stem from past issues in their life.

Concentration may be low as well because of the state of mind of the addict without the drug. The brain is trying to put itself back together so the brain is in a state of confusion without the drug. Low concentration is and can be a symptom that will pass quickly, depending on how motivated the addict is in their recovery. Getting a planner and planning your day will help in this process with less for the addict to think about. It will be easier when they know what to do and when to do it. Journaling will also help with getting your thoughts on track.

Headaches can pass quickly. In the beginning of the withdrawal stages; migraines are normal. A simple medication such as ibuprophen is a way to help ease the headaches in early withdrawals.

I always suggest that EVERY addict go and see a doctor and don't be afraid to let them know you are in early recovery and that you are in withdrawals. A doctor can always help pin point what medications if any are best for what you're going through.

In our addiction, our sleeping habits were erratic so getting our sleeping patterns back may be tough. Almost every addict suffers from insomnia. Going to bed at a certain time every night and waking up at a certain time is important. We have to retrain the brain as to when we will wake up and when we go to sleep. Many addicts in early recovery will sleep all day and night because the brain has no set schedule. Having insomnia at night when we should be sleeping is normal. Get a set schedule. I drank a tea called "sleepy time" that helped me sleep at night. But this won't work if you're sleeping all day. The trick to recovering your normal sleep schedule is making one and sticking to it. This may take time. Be patient and give your body time to catch up from the days and nights lost due to using drugs. Once again, consult your doctor and they can help you in this area as well.

Irritability is normal as well. This may be a tough one for loved ones because everyone around you may be caught in the cross fire.

Be aware of what your body is going through and how you react around others. Try to implement positive things in your life such as meetings, church, reading, writing, hobbies and exercise. This will help to get your self esteem back and that will help with your irritability.

Remember that your body has been through a lot and removing the drug/drugs is just the start. The body needs to restore itself. How quickly that will happen all depends on you and the work you put into healing yourself. Sitting and doing nothing all day is not recovery and you can and may just make things worse on yourself by doing nothing.

The physical withdrawal symptoms are nausea, vomiting, diarrhea, racing heartbeat, sweating, difficulty breathing, tightening of the chest, muscle tension, tremor, and palpitations. Many of these symptoms will pass after a few days.

It is very important to consult a doctor when coming off drugs. Doctors are trained to see and know things that we don't know. Each addict is different in their body chemistry and drug of choice. How the body reacts to different drugs in each individual addict is different. Size, weight, tolerance level, drug of choice and how long the addict has used, plays a huge role in how each addict will physically and mentally recover from the withdrawals in the safest way possible.

There also may be other underlying illnesses that have been with you for a while and have gone undetected. Why? Because addicts don't see the doctor regularly and they neglect their bodies. An addict may have medical issues and not even know it's there because of the masking that the drugs can do with certain illnesses.

Many addicts find out after they get clean that they have medical issues that come to surface when the drugs are removed. Some are caused by the drug use itself and some are not caused by the drugs at all.

The withdrawal symptoms are the toughest hurdle to make it through along with the PAWS. But I am here to encourage you that you can make it through as so many of us in recovery have done.

The trick is to want recovery more than you want the drugs. The key is to stay busy in your recovery. Uncomfortable things in your recovery will produce change that is needed in long term recovery. If going to a meeting or church or a Bible study is uncomfortable and you don't want to do it. You probably should do it, because it will bring about the change you are looking for long term sobriety.

The more time that passes in your recovery the easier it will get. Just don't try to do recovery by yourself. So many fail because they have no support system or people to talk to that understand what they are going through. Your body is great at healing itself but you have to help it along and by doing that you will retrain the brain to think of more positive things in your recovery. The brain is great at healing itself too, but it will take consistency from you and your willingness to heal in a healthy way.

When I first came into recovery, someone once told me that there is only one thing that you have to change in recovery and that one thing is everything!

Be willing to take suggestion from others. The one thing I notice with addicts in early recovery is that they think they know everything and they won't bend their way of thinking. They want to be right all the time.

There is no growth in being right. We grow when we remain teachable. It helps when we listen to others in recovery who have been on that road much longer.

If you listen to the suggestions I have made in this chapter, you can and will heal quickly and be on the road to recovery in no time at all. May God bless you and keep you until then.

Withdrawals In a Jail Cell

The cold cement floors,
Of a jail cell.
I grab a toilet paper roll,
To lay my head upon.
I feel the fire leaving my veins.
I feel the sickness overwhelming me.
The hot and cold chills that bind me.
I want to die.
What I would give for just one more hit.
To sooth the pain within me.

Breaking Chains ~ Paul Aragon

Why do I put myself through such misery?
I want to let go.
The fire in my veins controls me.
I want to sleep and never wake up.
In a fetus position on the cold floor.
There are others around me,
Just like me.
I am not alone.
I feel like my heart is without a home.
I reach out to something much bigger than me.
Can he hear me?
Or must I suffer the consequences of my disease, And
the Chains that bind me.
I am in hell,
Withdrawals in a jail cell.
I can't live in this insanity.
Only I, should control me.
The choices I make,
My selfish disease.
Hurts more than just me.

Poem by Paul C. Aragon

Chapter 9

My Loved One Is an Addict

It was two years before my third wife found out that she fell in love with a drug addict. She is a beautiful woman. Most men would die to have such a loyal and caring person in their life. But with drugs it is hard to see any further than the addiction itself. Addicts think only of themselves, even when kids and a loving wife pour their hearts out to make the addict happy. They stand by and try to help, only to have their heart stomped on time after time.

The kids usually don't know what's wrong with mom or dad, and the spouse is hoping that the addict will finally choose them over their addiction and not end up in bitter disappointment. They try and try to help their loved one get off drugs, but the forces of addiction usually prevail.

Broken hearts and broken families are left in turmoil. Moms and dads do the best they can to help, only to end up in fight after fight. The addicted loved one seems to be lost from reality and usually doesn't see the destruction. Drugs seem to have one sole purpose: to seek and destroy everything in its path. Promise after promise is broken time after time. Things go missing from homes just to support the habit. Loved ones want to be the one to save the addict, and every story they hear about addiction can't break their spirit from trying to be the one to reach the addicted loved one.

Years and years are wasted. The loved one's life is put on hold only to have their hopes squashed by another relapse. Night after night of lost sleep hoping not to get the dreaded phone call that says your addicted loved one is dead. What can you do different than any other parent, husband or wife to help the addicted loved one? You maybe reading this book for that reason only, to slip into the mind of an addict and find the key that makes you the hero in your addicted loved one's life. I can't blame you for that; many loved ones wish the same. You may be an addict reading this book in hopes of finding the key to letting go of drugs forever. I hope to be able to save you lost years and time through the pages of this book, and I hope that I can set your heart at ease and give you knowledge you may not have. I commend you for you efforts.

But let me be honest with you right out of the gate. You will never be the hero. You will never be able to help your loved one off drugs. In the chapter in this book titled "The Recovery Process," you will learn what real recovery is, and how an addict can obtain it.

As a loved one there are things you can do. Some of them you may not like to hear and other things may give you hope. The most important thing you must know is that if your life gets off track because of a loved one's addiction, you will render yourself useless to your addicted loved one.

I have been in so many relationships where I was yelled at, degraded, condemned, made fun of, talked down upon; fight after fight with nothing but repeated words in hopes of winning the conversation. You will never win over an addict by acting as they act. If you're the sane one and the one who doesn't do dope, then you should be in control of every conversation and you should also be in control of your tone and what you say and how you respond to an addict. Remember they're on drugs, and they think they are right all the time. They will try to push the blame on you or something else in their life that caused them to be the way they are. So is it helpful to show your anger to them? It all depends on how you do it. You can do it without raising your voice and without pointing fingers. When you're talking to the addicted loved, one it is best to remember this: *Always keep yourself in a position to be helpful.* You don't want to push them from you, but you don't want to let them walk on you either.

There are loved ones who try too hard and give and give to the addict. Those people usually become enablers and even worse, codependents. If this happens you will push that addict so far from you, you will have your own addiction to worry about – codependency.

I have always said that tough love is the best love when it comes to an addicted loved one because it puts recovery on the addict where it belongs. No one else is responsible for recovery but the addict. Once you start trying to help the addict, they usually will use you until your wheels fall off. Then what happens is you turn your back on them and the relationship is broken.

So would you like an example?

Here goes: "Honey I love you, and I want what's best for you, but I can no longer allow you to live in this home. I can no longer watch you day after day abuse your dad and me (or your children and me). When you're ready to get help we will be there to support you, but you have to do it and want it for yourself."

An addict may hear this and come back a week or two later and say, "I am ready I want to come home." Don't do it. You will only wreak havoc on yourself and your family. Once again, in the next chapter about recovery, you will read more on what recovery is and how they may obtain it. But it is never wise to bring an addict in the house during full addiction having the kids see them during withdrawal. A loved one should never put themselves in a position to see a spouse, a son or daughter in full withdrawal. You may say, that's what parents do or that's what a wife is supposed to do, but it is not wise. If you don't know addiction, it may be horrific no matter the drug. An addict will steal and rob from you just to get their next fix, never really comprehending what they're doing or the consequences. They just want to feel normal again.

What happens in the brain of an addict is more than you could understand. Tough love is really just being there for support, saying "good job" and "I am so proud of you." You can let them come over to get a meal or even wash their clothes, but don't give them money and don't let them stay.

Not every addict needs to hit a rock bottom, but an addict has to want recovery. They really have to want to stop; even then it has to be on their terms, and it usually doesn't go in sync with what you think they should be doing. So it is best to put clear boundaries in place and stick by them. Many marriages have ended up in divorce because one parent doesn't want to give up on their addicted loved one. The marriage itself is being neglected and torn apart because of differences of opinions on the matter. One parent always gets sick of their crap while the other one hangs on to hope. It is ok to have hope, but not at the cost of your children, marriages or families. Families always will get put on hold; time passes so quickly that it ends up being years of neglecting yourself and family, while the addict spins out of control and has no idea of the destruction in the home.

I had stomped three wives' hearts into the ground. I loved them and never intended to hurt them, but the power drugs had over me was too great. My third wife tried and tried to be there for me, to help me and to support me. My addiction would bring out a new problem in my marriage–

codependency. My wife had fought for many years to save this marriage for the man she loved. She should have taken the advice of those close to her and ran as fast as she could. Could it ever be worth all the years of pain I caused?

In and out of the house more times than I could count, one day she had enough. She came home from a church function and sat me down in the bedroom. Normally when she kicked me out it was a big fight in front of the kids. I would go stomping out, and return a few days or weeks later. But this time it was different. We sat on the bed and she said in a soft voice as tears flowed from her eyes, "I love you so much, but I am broken and it can't be fixed anymore." She continued by saying, "I have tried and tried, but my heart can't take any more. Our family has fallen apart, and I need you to leave. You and I are over. I am done. You can see the kids if you get clean and can prove it to me. But if I think you're using, you will not be allowed around the kids."

So I left the home, and continued to use. In and out of over 30 sober living homes through the years, I thought I was destined to die an addict. I would find out later on that my wife had a few churches praying for me. Every friend she knew was also praying for me. She even posted it on the internet; she must have had hundreds praying for me. It wasn't long before I was picked up on a no-bail warrant. I was going to prison. Be careful what you pray for because God always hears our prayers.

The judge gave me one last chance and I was put in an outpatient program called Drug Court. I was being tested 5 days a week and had no room for error. The judge told me that if I had one violation I would go to prison for a long time. The judge was done with me, too. Those hundreds of prayers saved my life and my marriage, and have helped me become the man that I am today.

Addiction is tough for those who don't know it. It is a very scary place. But remember it is a choice that the addict made to use drugs, and it's up to them to stop on their own. An addict will do everything in the world to make you feel guilty for not helping them, giving them money or not letting them come home. Stand by your boundaries and have them in place.

The Mother's Cry

I can't tell you the pain a parent feels,
When they have to say:
My loved one is an addict.
Where did I go wrong?
The sleepless nights,
I wait for a phone call.
Will it be the police again?
Or will the morgue call this time?
I remember when my baby was born.
So sweet,
So quiet,
So full of joy.
Untouched by this sinful world.
What can a mother do?
How can I help?
I tried and tried,
But my baby has turned into something,
I cannot recognize.
Their voice has changed.
It is like a demon within them.
I don't have such strength.
I pray without ceasing.
I won't stop.
My tears are drained.
I sleep well,
When my baby is in a jail cell.
I know it's sad.

Breaking Chains ~ Paul Aragon

But it is the only time I find rest.
Because I know they are safe.
I just want to hold my baby,
let them know everything will be ok.
If they would only let go of the poison that has taken
my baby from me.
Please help me.

Poem by Paul C. Aragon

Chapter 10

The Recovery Process

I have spent many years trying to get clean from drugs, only to end up in disappointment after disappointment. Drugs are a monster. They are so hard to shake when caught in its grasp. People who have never been addicted have the hardest time understanding why addicts don't just stop. I wish it was as easy as that. All I can say is that there is so much that goes on in the brain of an addict that it is more than just saying, "I quit."

Everything we do in life the brain learns, such as brushing our teeth. Parents tell us as kids and remind us everyday to brush our teeth. After years of this it becomes second nature to brush our teeth. We go to the bathroom, take out the toothbrush and we brush without even thinking about it. This is because it has been permanently embedded in the brain. Although addiction takes place in a totally different area of the brain, the memory part of the brain never forgets a memory.

The chemicals in the midbrain, where addiction takes place, is even more complicated. If the brain never forgets a memory, and you add to it the "feel good" information sent to the brain from the release of those chemicals, the brain will always ask for more.

Addiction can be worse when you begin to use drugs as a teenager, because the brain isn't fully developed. The brain is still processing emotions and how to deal with each emotion. When you add drugs into the process, the brain will learn to need that drug through all those years of different emotions and feelings. The drug itself tricks the brain into releasing these chemicals in the midbrain and an overabundance of these chemicals are released, more than in a natural pleasure. When you take the drug away, the brain is thrown into a horrific state of being without the overabundance of these chemicals and the addict experiences anxiety and depression.

I have tried to get clean more times than I could count. I will share with you in this chapter what it finally took and how recovery took its roots. Because there are many ups and downs the addict will go through in the process of getting off drugs, many fall back into addiction because the process is too much for them to handle.

Many are reading this book in hopes of finding an easy way to get off drugs or an easy out. There isn't one! Recovery is simple, but it is not easy. I will share with you the methods that work. But I would highly urge you to take notice that the key word is WORK! I will use the word **work** many times in this chapter. Take notice of it and highlight it if you have to.

In our addiction we worked hard to get and stay high. We worked hard to keep our stories straight and our brains moving as we justified and rationalized our bad behaviors. We worked 24 hours a day in our addiction and no addict will deny that. Would any less be sufficient for **long-term** recovery? The answer is: NO! I have seen many people with years in recovery relapse because they stopped working their program of recovery. They got lazy because they thought they "got this" thing called recovery. But I will tell you now that once you think you've *got this*, you have already lost it.

My recovery really took its roots when I decided to take it seriously and became willing to put everything I had into it. Recovery became the most important thing in my life. I came to realize that if I didn't have my recovery, I wouldn't have a job, my family, my car or anything thing that I owned without it. So when you put recovery in that perspective, recovery must always come before everything in your life. Without it you will have nothing.

Many people get a job and a car, but they get so busy with work that they ignore their recovery. Soon their cravings and thoughts of using come back and the addict succumbs. I hope you have your highlighter out and are marking these key points that I am giving you; they are priceless when it comes to recovery.

What is the best method of recovery and what is best for you? The choice is yours. I will explain a few, but keep in mind that if you're taking one off the table because it requires too much *work*, you're looking for an easy way and there is no easy way when it comes to long-term recovery. Keep an open mind and be willing to try anything because this is your life. This is your recovery. No great rewards go without hard work. The harder you work, the greater the rewards.

The last chapter of this book is titled "About the Author." That is my story; and when you read it, you will see how hard I worked in my recovery and the great rewards that came with my hard work.

One of the most successful paths of recovery are the 12 step programs. There are even faith based 12 step programs that work well and the success rate is very high. Many people have done drugs so long that they need to be taken away from their world and placed in an inpatient rehabilitation center. Many of these rehabs will focus on you and your recovery. They prescribe medications for onset depression when getting these drugs out of your system. These rehabs will also introduce you to the 12 step programs and even have church services for those who desire that. If you have a faith, hold onto it and let it be the foundation of you recovery. Rehabs usually will take a person in and keep you anywhere from 30 days to 4 months on average. There are some that will take you longer. The important thing to remember is ***don't leave earlier than recommended.*** Your recovery must start with completing something. We fail in our addiction, so we must be successful in our recovery.

Where I see most people fail is when they get out. They are like lost children and have nowhere to go, don't know what to do and they end up back on the streets using in no time. During your last few weeks, get with your appointed counselor and find out where recovery homes or sober living homes are so you have a supportive place to go that is safe. Many people want to go straight home to the wife and kids. They don't work a program and the addict returns. Give yourself at least a few months in well structured sober living home that requires you to go to meetings. This way you can get used to your new life with others in recovery. You can get to know new friends in recovery and build a support system before going back into the real world. The world is tough enough for non-addicts. Being an addict new in recovery can be overwhelming; gradually slip back into life, prepare yourself well, and don't jump right into it.

The 12 step programs have meetings all over. Many people like to go every day, but others may only go three days a week. You can determine what is best for you by how you're feeling. If you're stressed or depressed, or having thoughts of using, you may need more meetings. When I got clean I went to meetings six days a week for two years and church every Sunday. When you go to these meetings, you will hear people talking about their sponsors. A sponsor is a person who is almost like a mentor and will take you through the 12 steps. The 12 steps are designed to change your life. They are so awesome at changing the old you into the person you were intended to be. I believe that everyone in the world, addict or not, should take the 12 steps because of how they turn a selfish person into a *selfless* person.

You can find sponsors at meetings. Just ask a person you see who really seems to be working a program if they will sponsor you. You can usually tell by the way they share at meetings that they are knowledgeable in the 12 step program. That's how you seek them out.

If the 12 step program is the route you choose, don't be lazy in the steps; work hard on your steps. If one day goes by where you aren't working on an assignment that your sponsor gave you, that is what I call dead time. Work hard on your steps. Some people will say "take your time on your steps" and I think that this is bad advice. We never took our time in our addiction, so we don't take our time in saving our life either. We go after it and work hard on it. Go at a pace where you are working the steps hard but at a steady pace. I have seen people that were only on step 2 at a year in recovery, and to me that is just pure laziness. I had taken all 12 steps in less than 60 days and was sponsoring other addicts at five months in recovery.

Many people don't want to take the 12 step route. If this is you, and you have a faith, this is what I suggest: if you don't already have a faith based church, find one that makes you feel comfortable. It should feel like home to you. Don't just go on Sundays and call that recovery – it's not. Go to the pastor and tell him you want to get involved in the church, and that you want to volunteer in a ministry. It could be any ministry: children's ministry, an outreach ministry; coffee ministry; or become a greeter, an usher, or volunteer at the information center. There are so many places you can serve in the church. I personally have served in many and have started several ministries as well. I also recommend finding a weekly Bible study. Go to all the events and functions the church has to offer. Don't just be a Sunday church person, but get involved in the body of the church.

Get to know people because they will become the support system that you need. By getting involved in the church, you will get to know many people quickly and you will make many friends. Everything you just read I personally did, including the 12 step program. I also went to school and got my diploma and some other degrees. Stay busy in your recovery. There should be no time in your schedule to play the tapes of your drug addiction days in your head.

Follow your dreams and change your life. I got clean at 42 years old. I have gone further than I ever thought I would go. These last few years I have even taught the Sunday service at my church a few times and it was amazing. I never thought that I would go that far in my recovery, but I did. Life is so good for me today.

There will be challenges in your recovery because life is in session, and it doesn't stop because you're clean. We just take recovery one day at a time and one problem at a time. But we stay busy in our recovery.

Keep a balance, however, in your personal life and in your recovery. In other words, have healthy boundaries in place so you're not taking too much time away from your family life. Have fun. I joined a softball team just to do something for me. It was so much fun having my family come watch me play.

Start a faith-based meeting at your church after you have acquired some time in recovery. Grow and expand your life and don't sit still.

There is also a great faith-based 12 step program out there called Celebrate Recovery. This is another great way to take the steps and meet people of the same faith. I was the leader of Celebrate Recovery for a few years at my church and I just loved it. I have taken the 12 steps in Narcotics Anonymous, Alcoholics Anonymous, and Celebrate Recovery. I have changed my life so dramatically that those who knew me in my addiction are in awe of who I am today.

If you're sitting home doing nothing and expect to change your life, it isn't going to happen. Don't sit around with the "Oh poor me" attitude. Get up and do something to change your life. Those people that just quit on their own and don't change their life usually go back to drugs. Why? Just taking away the drug doesn't change anything. The addict is still there. If you want to get rid of the addict in you, then put work into it.

White knuckling it isn't recovery. It's just an addict without the dope. All the people that see you and know you haven't changed your life are just waiting for you to go back to drugs. Your loved ones that see you off drugs can see that you haven't changed. You're the same angry, selfish person that you were in your addiction. Is that what you want? Or would you like your kids, your family, parents and loved ones to see a new you with a new sparkle in your eye – a person with compassion, kindness and love in your heart. Then you are going to have to work for it.

Recovery is a journey, a life-long journey that has ups and downs as we continue to grow each day. I always tell the people I work with in recovery that if you are asked to do something in recovery that is uncomfortable, and you really don't want to do it, then you probably should. Recovery is uncomfortable because it is about change. Change is uncomfortable because we are stepping outside our comfort zone. We are stepping outside of what we know and are reaching new heights.

Most addicts don't know what it's like to succeed, so they self-sabotage themselves and purposely fail so they don't have to have the feeling of *I failed trying.* It's easier for them to make the choice to go out and use rather than try. They think it's easier to just choose to fail than to try and make it through the withdrawals and the tough times in recovery. But the truth is that every addict out there has really tough times in their addiction. They made it through *those* tough times, so how much greater would they be if they applied that in their recovery? Seriously, do you realize how much crap we addicts put ourselves through? We put ourselves through so much crap and hell here on earth on a daily basis and we get through that. Yes, we get through it by using drugs, but inside us we make it through each day regardless. If we used the efforts that we put into drugs and applied it in our recovery, there would be so many more success stories!!

Each and every addict has brilliance in them. They just have to choose to be brilliant. Every addict also has greatness in them; they just have to choose to be great. We also have to commit ourselves to the choice of applying that brilliance and greatness in our lives.

DIVORCING DRUGS

The papers are signed.
I did love you at times;
I am not going to lie.
Which is all the more reason,
I need to say goodbye.
The pain you put me through,
Broken promises,
And the same old lies,
Wasted years with you,
Chasing that one high,
I chose you over my family,
How could I have been so blind?
All the years I wasted with you,
You're a demon in disguise.
I am not even sure what I saw in you.
I should have run when everyone told me to.
That is why I am divorcing you.
It's over, I don't want you anymore.
You were a mistake in my life,
And now a closed door.
It's time to find out who I can be,
With all of God's power inside me.
So now it is time,

Breaking Chains ~ Paul Aragon

For me to say goodbye.
But this time I will do it,
And I will not cry.

Poem by Paul C. Aragon

Chapter 11

Words from My Heart

I hope this book has brought hope to you and your family. I pray that it has given you a more clear understanding of drugs and the power that addiction can have over you and your loved ones.

Addiction doesn't only affect the addict, but it affects the lives of everyone around the addict. Many addicts say, "I am not hurting anyone but myself." This is so far from the truth, as you have read within these pages.

Drug addiction does affect everyone around the addict as they see the change take place in the addict's life and they sit back and watch their world crumble. It is heart wrenching for a child, spouse, family member, or friends to sit back and watch the destruction take place while the addict sees nothing wrong with their behavior.

Family members and friends feel hopeless as they try everything in their power to reach out and help the addict, and they only push them further away from hope.

If you have read this book thoroughly, you may have noticed that I repeated certain things over and over. I did that intentionally because the more we read or hear things of importance and value, the more it will sink in.

I strongly suggest that you read this book again; and when you do, use a highlighter pen to mark the important sections that relate to you and what you are going through.

As with anything in life, we can't be narrow-minded. We must keep an open mind so that if what we are doing isn't working, then it is time to change our tactics. I have written within these pages that anything that is uncomfortable for us to do may be the very thing we need to do.

No loved one wants to give up on the addict, and I don't think anyone should give up on their loved one. But there comes a point where there is nothing more you can do, and it may be time to let the addict figure it out on their own.

Tough love is uncomfortable because nobody wants to intentionally turn their back on the ones they love. But in many cases tough love may just save your loved one's life. Will they be resentful towards you? Yes, but it will get them that much closer to seeing that their world is falling apart and that they are in need of change. Should tough love be given to every addict? No, each case is different; but if you see that you are enabling the addict and their behavior, then you may be prolonging the process.

Family members need to heal as well, and I suggest that every loved one involved with an addict seek help as well. Alanon meetings are a great way for you to get support and a better understanding of addiction. Alanon meetings also provide you with the opportunity to share what you're going through with others in a healthy way. It will give others opportunity to help you through this so you don't have to go through it alone.

If you are an addict reading this book, I strongly suggest that you read this book again closely, and know that you are valuable in this world. You have the power just as much as millions of addicts in recovery do, to change your life. You are not worthless or a piece of crap or even a lowlife. Your addiction would love you to believe that because it wants you in its grip.

I have seen the lowest down addict pick themselves up and change their life, but they wanted that change and would go to any lengths to get it. Recovery must become a way of life for you and one that you cherish with every passing day.

I lost my family and my friends and everyone around me because I couldn't be trusted any more. I burnt bridge after bridge because of my addiction. I was homeless, jobless, friendless and alone at my lowest point of my addiction.

I remember one day I was out of money, out of drugs and had been kicked out of my home. I was sleeping in back of a supermarket and it had begun to rain. I was curled up in a ball cold alone and in withdrawals. As the rain began to come down I could smell that I was lying in urine from people who had been there before me. I was staring at this piece of gum that was grounded into the cement and had turned black. The piece of gum reminded me of where I was in my life. I felt just like that piece of gum. Right next to the piece of gum was a cigarette butt that was smashed to the ground and as flat as it could possibly be. I looked at it as well and thought this is my life, smashed down as far as it can go, and I was ready to die with the smell of urine all around me.

Was this my life? Was this what it was going to be, or was I going to stand up and make the change that I needed to change my life? When was

I going to stop blaming everyone around me? When was I going to stop blaming my addiction on my past?

Some of the reasons we start drugs may be valid, but how long will we let our past consume us? There comes a time when those legitimate reasons for starting drugs become an excuse to continue the bad behavior. The drugs stop working and become work in itself just to stay high. Then our addiction pushes the people in our lives away from us and cause more destruction and heartache.

Some of the things we go through as children can be horrific and can play a big part in our addiction. But if we allow the things we went through to keep us in our addiction, are we not letting those things still have power over us? Are we still going to let those things control us by continuing our addiction? There comes a time when we have to let go of the things that people have done to us. Otherwise we are still letting them have power over us and we are letting them still control us by continuing our addiction.

Find a way to let that hurt go or you will never get to a point where you can heal from that pain. I personally went to many therapy sessions to help me with what I went through as a child. Yes, it was sad what I went through, and I hated God and everyone around me for not protecting me as a child. But I could never find recovery until I was able to let those things I went through go. It took me over thirty years to let those things go; and just look at all the damage it caused. I had to break those chains that bound me for so many years.

Those chains had bound me for so many years because I was unwilling to find forgiveness in my heart and let it go. We don't find forgiveness for the other person, but we find it for ourselves so we can change the rage and break those chains that bind us.

No person is greater than the next. Everyone has greatness in them and the ability to be all they can be in this life.

Never in a million years would I have thought I would be where I am today and have accomplished what I have done in my life. I never would have believed that I could be where I am today. I had caused so much damage that I thought I would be alone for the rest of my life. But that wasn't my story. My family loves me today and has found forgiveness because of the changes I have made in my life. And even if they didn't find forgiveness and they were apart from me, I would still be the man I am today. Not everyone is going to forgive you because of your past; that's on them

Breaking Chains ~ Paul Aragon

not you. Don't believe otherwise. If you tried to make amends and they won't forgive you then let it go. That is their side of the street not yours. Your side of the street is clean if you have done everything in your power to change your life and are continuing to work on you.

Don't let anyone make you feel different than what you have become. Some people hold on to bitterness and hate; that alone is a sickness that they will blame on you. It goes much deeper than that, and that is something they need to look at, not you.

People who stay angry at you because of your past are no different than you were in your addiction. They are blaming someone else for how they feel and what they do when they have the power to change it.

They may see you changing your life and hold onto bitterness out of fear that you might relapse and continue hurting them. It may just be their defense mechanism to protect their heart. In fact, all it is doing is hurting them further by distancing themselves from you because of what happened in the past.

Some people just need time to heal because of what addicts have done to them; others need therapy and need to change themselves. Trust me;

addicts aren't the only ones in this world that need to change. We all need change.

Anyone taking the time to read this book has taken that first step in change and has the ability to heal as long as they don't read this book with their own set opinions. We all must always keep an open mind and an open heart. Trust God if you have faith; Go to Him in all that you do, and ask yourself what would God do in this situation? It may be different than what you would do and how you would react.

If you are a loved one reading this book, I can understand the pain that addicts cause in their addiction to those they love. You may have so much anger inside you that you can't find it in your heart to forgive them. I can so understand that and have compassion for you and all that you have been through. But if your loved one is trying to change their life and is working hard, give them a little at a time. Don't let the addiction and the pain caused from addiction consume you even when the addiction is gone. Don't give addiction that power. Let go of the hurt and give yourself time to heal. Let forgiveness be a part of your goal and try to get to a place where you can do that. Don't let anger and hate consume you.

I will pray for all the readers of this book to heal and find recovery in their life and in their family. Never give up hope, because hope is what God gives to all of us. The best tool I have found is prayer. Prayer saved my life, so pray without ceasing.

If anyone would like to talk to me personally, you can reach me on my recovery page on Facebook, *Breaking Chains: Chronicles of a Meth Addict*

https://www.facebook.com/BreakingChainsChroniclesOfaMethAddict

May God keep you until then.

Dear Mom

I am sorry for the pain I caused.
I never knew what I put you through.
The sleepless nights,
You stayed up worrying about me.
Never knowing if I was dead or alive,
Or what happened to me,
As my mom, I know you tried to protect me,
I closed that door,
And said "all I am hurting is me,"
My addiction kept tears in your eyes.

Breaking Chains ~ Paul Aragon

The things I stole from you,
When you tried to help me.
I was blind, but now I see.
How much I love you,
And how much you mean to me.
Now I have my sobriety,
And clarity,
I hold close to me my recovery,
And what it means to me.
I apologize for all I have done.
I owe a lifetime of amends to you,
And every day I am clean,
I will give that to you.
I know it will take time for you to heal,
Take all the time you need,
To see in me,
This time "it's for real".
I will work real hard,
So you can trust me.
I will become the person I know I can be.
Your child,
Always your baby!
I love you!!

Poem by Paul C. Aragon

About the Author

This book is written for addicts and their families in crisis of addiction. This book is also for those in recovery with questions about recovery and addiction. I cover many areas of concern when it comes to trying to understand addiction and recovery. My dream since early recovery has always been to write a book about my addiction. I never realized that in my recovery I would go to school and spend many years working in the substance abuse field. This book has turned out to be more than I ever dreamed. It is not only a book that shares my personal experiences, but also my knowledge in the addiction field.

My name is Paul. I used drugs and alcohol for 31 years. I drank my first beer at nine years old and smoked my first joint at 12 years old. I became an IV drug user at the age of 15. Also at the age of 15, I got my first juvenile jacket (court file) because of burglary. The second juvenile offense was for burglary as well, trying to support my drug habit. I got my first adult jacket (court file) at the age of 17. Because I was a runaway, the court considered me as an adult. I was sent to adult jail for the first time at 17 years of age.

I have been locked up more times than I can count; all of my charges were in some way linked to drugs by me being irresponsible and just not caring. I have been to many treatment programs: inpatient programs, outpatient programs, over 30 sober living homes, and even a few different psychiatric wards. I have had 4 different 12 step sponsors and countless times where I just couldn't stay off drugs. I have lost 3 wives because of drugs, and I got the third one back because of recovery. I have hurt stepchildren so badly that a few won't even talk to me to this day; others that are still in my life are still healing from the pain I caused.

My drug use came to an end at the age of 42 by an angry judge. At that time I had prior felonies for other drug charges. I didn't do the drug diversion classes that they offered me and a "No Bail" warrant was put out for me. They caught me the second time with drugs behind my drug dealer's house in a back alley. I tried to run but there was nowhere to go. I was taken to jail on numerous felony charges, possession, paraphernalia, resisting arrest, and my prior felonies with a no bail warrant still on my back. Metaphorically speaking, I was nailed to a cross.

With a two-year-old boy at home and a newborn that was only a few months old, I was afraid I would never see them again. When I got to court, the judge told the bailiff to send me back to jail so I could sit and think about my life and where it was going. She was so mad at me because she knew about my family and the pain I had caused my wife and kids.

"I need to really think about what I am going to do with you, Mr. Aragon. I am fed up with you and what you are doing with your life and what you're doing to your family," she said. She wouldn't even let me talk. "Get him out of here," she said to the bailiff.

When I went back to court weeks later, the judge told me that she would give me one last chance; and she put me in drug court. I was tested for drugs five days a week, and if I missed one test or if I tested positive for drugs, I was going to prison for a very long time.

Drug court is an extensive outpatient program; I had to go to 3 classes a day, five days a week. I also was required to go to court every two weeks so the judge could check my progress from all of my counselors. I had so many classes that I could only work a part-time job to support my family.

The craving for more drugs was unbearable and for the first time, I reached out to God and asked him if he was really there, that I needed him and his help. I told God, "I will do anything you ask me to. Just remove the obsession for me to drink and use drugs." I would get that opportunity. I moved into a well-structured sober living home when I got out of jail. I got a sponsor and began to work the 12 steps of A.A. I tried the N.A. program at first, but I was extremely triggered just being around other addicts; so I decided that maybe I would try A.A.

I took the 12 steps in about 3 months. I moved through them like a drowning man. If you're an addict reading this and you're against the 12 steps, DON'T put this book down. I believe there are many ways to recover and you will read some of them within the pages of this book. Don't knock anything because it requires work. The 12 steps will truly change your life if you find the right person to take you through them. Be willing to try anything in your recovery; don't count anything out because you're too lazy to do it. This is your life you're talking about. I tried anything and everything that was put in front of me with drugs, so I had to do the same with my recovery. If someone suggested it, I tried it; and with the best of my ability I did it to the fullest.

Within my first 30 days of recovery, I went to a church that I had attended even on dope. I told them I was trying to stay clean and that I needed something to do. This was about the time I truly gave my heart to Christ. I needed a place to volunteer just so I could stay out of my own head and stay busy. The following Sunday the pastor gave me my new position.

I became an usher where I met many people that were just like me – people looking to fill a hole in their hearts; people who yearned for something more and were seeking a real purpose in life.

At about a year clean and sober, I also went back to school to get my high school diploma and graduated with a 4.0. By that time I had completed my year and a half of court ordered intense outpatient therapy.

Within my first two years of recovery, I had taken all 12 steps in the N.A. program and in Celebrate Recovery, a Christ-centered group that teaches the 12 steps biblically.

After a year I began teaching in the children's ministry and over time I taught every grade from nursery school to high school kids. I became involved in many ministries and outreach ministries throughout the church. After two years in recovery I was asked to lead and teach the Celebrate Recovery group at the church. I also was a secretary at a local A.A. meeting on Thursday mornings and even had my own H&I (hospitals and institutions) panel at an inpatient rehabilitation center on Saturday mornings.

I then started going to school to be Substance Abuse Counselor and within four years of recovery, I received my R.A.S (Registered Abuse Specialist) certification. I also obtained two certifications from a separate school in Christian Substance Abuse counseling, a CSAC I and a CSAC II. I also earned 156 units in Christian Ministry from the same school.

I was sponsoring many men in the drug court program and the judge knew it and was impressed with my change. Months after I completed, my P.O. had lunch with the judge and coincidently my name was brought up by my P.O. He shared with the judge how unbelievable I was doing and how impressed he was with my progress in recovery.

The judge told my P.O. that she wanted to see me back in court. I received a call from my P.O. who told me the judge wanted to see me in court. I wasn't sure why and I was worried. I was the first one called up to see the judge that day. She asked me if all the things I was doing in recovery were true and I stated that they were. She asked me to share with the court everything I was doing and I told her everything you just read.

She then stood up on the bench, motioning for all the people in court, including the bailiff, to stand up. At that point I was given a standing ovation. As tears of appreciation rolled down my face, the judge continued to tell me I would have a hard time getting a job with two felonies on my back. One felony she had already removed for the completion of Drug Court. I answered to her that God would take care of me and that I wasn't too worried about it. She replied, "Today God is taking care of that." I am dismissing your felonies and your record is clean as of today.

I assume she took care of this days before I entered the courtroom. I cried like never before. She stated that I was the most extreme case of a man of change and that she was so impressed with me that she wanted the addicts in court to see what it looks like for a person to chase their recovery and the rewards that would follow.

She asked me to come back and speak to the addicts in her courtroom anytime I wanted to. I did that several times after that day and was the only person allowed to do so in her courtroom to this very day.

I have worked at inpatient facilities and outpatient facilities; I have worked with juveniles and I have travelled all over California and even some places in Oregon teaching and sharing recovery at many places. Many years later in my recovery I have even obtained a second nationwide certification in Substance Abuse Counseling (CADC I) and a state Recovery Mentor Certification as well. I just recently even picked up a certification from the Oregon State Department of Corrections to volunteer mentoring men in prison.

I am a leader at my church. I have also been so blessed to play percussion for my church on the worship team. I have started ministries at my church and have even been so blessed to teach the main service at my church on Sunday mornings a few times. My dream has always been to write a book that can help addicts and their families suffering from addiction, and this is that book.

Through hard work and perseverance, I have become an awesome dad to my kids with the help of about 4 parenting classes along the way. I am working hard on my marriage on a daily basis, and this infant man in life is continuing to find out more about who I am as a man and as a man of God. It's a lot of work, but the rewards keep coming. I have many storms that roll by from time to time, but that is when I check my gratitude list and I wade through that storm using my recovery and using the tools I have picked up along the way. The more a person puts into their recovery, the more they will receive from it. The trick is this: I chase my recovery like I did my dope and still do till this very day.

I give God all the honor and glory and praise for all my achievements and my achievements to come. He is my Rock and my Redeemer and my Savior. It is through Him that I am truly freed from my drug addiction.

Special Acknowledgments

To my brother Skip, thank you for helping me with the editing of this book.

To Zak Graham for the cover design, thank you my brother in Christ.

Special thanks to all the fans of "Breaking Chains: Chronicles of a Meth Addict"
http://www.facebook.com/BreakingChainsChroniclesOfaMethAddict
for all your encouragement, love and support!! May God bless you in all you touch and all you do!!

Made in the USA
San Bernardino, CA
12 July 2017